BIBLE CHARACTERS AND DOCTRINES

Uzziah to Daniel

E. M. BLAIKLOCK, M.A., D.Litt.

The Life of Christ

H. L. ELLISON, B.A., B.D.

DISCARD

WILLIAM B. EERDMANS PUBLISHING COMPANY
GRAND RAPIDS, MICHIGAN

© 1973 Scripture Union
First published 1973
First U.S.A. edition June 1973
Library of Congress Catalog Number: 72-189855
ISBN 0-8028-1463-8

SCRIPTURE UNION IN NORTH AMERICA

U. S. A.:   38 Garrett Road, Upper Darby,
             Pennsylvania 19082
Canada: 5 Rowanwood Avenue, Toronto 5,
             Ontario

Printed in the United States of America.

INTRODUCTION

Each volume of Bible Characters and Doctrines is divided into the right number of sections to make daily use possible, though dates are not attached to the sections because of the books' continuing use as a complete set of character studies and doctrinal expositions. The study for each day is clearly numbered and the Bible passage to be read is placed alongside it.

Sections presenting the characters and doctrines alternate throughout each book, providing balance and variety in the selected subjects. At the end of each section there is a selection of questions and themes for further study related to the material covered in the preceding readings.

Each volume will provide material for one quarter's use, with between 91 and 96 sections. Where it is suggested that two sections should be read together in order to fit the three-month period, they are marked with an asterisk.

The scheme will be completed in four years. Professor F. M. Blaiklock, who writes all the character studies, will work progressively through the Old and New Testament records. Writers of the doctrinal sections contribute to a pattern of studies drawn up by the Rev. Geoffrey Grogan, Principal of the Bible Training Institute, Glasgow, in his capacity as Co-ordinating Editor. A chart overleaf indicates how the doctrinal sections are planned.

In this series biblical quotations are normally taken from the RSV unless otherwise identified. Occasionally Professor Blaiklock provides his own translation of the biblical text.

DOCTRINAL STUDY SCHEME

	Year 1	Year 2	Year 3	Year 4
First Quarter	The God who Speaks	Man and Sin	The Work of Christ	The Kingdom and the Church
Second Quarter	God in His World	Law and Grace	Righteousness in Christ	The Mission of the Church
Third Quarter	The Character of God	The Life of Christ	Life in Christ	The Church's Ministry and Ordinances
Fourth Quarter	The Holy Trinity	The Person of Christ	The Holy Spirit	The Last Things

DOCTRINAL STUDIES
THE LIFE OF CHRIST

CHARACTER STUDIES
UZZIAH TO DANIEL

7

THE LIFE OF CHRIST

Introduction

Even allowing for the fact that there is another study-book on the teaching of Christ, it is impossible to cover all the known details of the life of Christ in one study-book. To avoid undue subjectivity, the sections chosen for treatment were not picked by the author, so he is not responsible if your favourite story is not to be found here.

Though technical points have not been eschewed, where the understanding of the passage seemed to depend on them, they have been kept to a minimum. Equally no attempt has been made to supplant the Bible dictionary and atlas. Those wishing for more detailed exposition are referred (in ascending order of magnitude) to *The New Bible Commentary* (Revised, I.V.P.), *A new Testament Commentary* (Pickering & Inglis), the respective volumes of the *Tyndale New Testament Commentaries* (I.V.P.).

At the head of each section parallel passages are noted. Those wishing to study such passages together with the main text will find *Gospel Parallels*, published by Nelson, most convenient. Since I do not wish to be quoted as the authority, I have preferred to mention other translations as my authority, where I have left the RSV. Among the abbreviations used are Jer.B. = Jerusalem Bible, TEV = Today's English Version, also NBD = New Bible Dictionary, NBC = New Bible Commentary.

The main stress throughout the comments has been on the humanity of our Lord, to draw out the impression He made on His contemporaries. For this reason the name Jesus, without any additions, has normally been preferred.

THE LIFE OF CHRIST

Jesus' Birth and Childhood

1 : The Preparation

Luke 1.5–25

God's ability to create from nothing, to make light shine out of darkness, mesmerizes some, so they find no room for the slow and unerring unfolding of His plans. Jesus was born when 'the time had fully come' (Gal. 4.4); if He came to His own home (John 1.11), i.e. the world, we should remember that He had both made it and controlled its development from the first, and above all, from the time of Abraham.

Here we are introduced to two products of the preparation, 'righteous . . . blameless', yet men privately pointed the finger of scorn at them, for they were childless; both being over sixty, all hope had gone. Yet another thing seemed to indicate Zechariah's being under Divine displeasure. All priestly service was fixed by lot; the burning of incense was considered so supreme that no one was chosen more than once in his life. Though he was one of the oldest functioning priests this lot had never fallen on Zechariah. Now the one day brought honour and promise, the former so that the latter might more easily be believed. Zechariah knew that the one standing by the altar (11) must be an angel, not because of his form, which was human, but because only an officiating priest could enter the Temple. For Gabriel see Dan. 8.16; 9.21.

Gabriel's message rose to a climax: your prayer is heard, a son John (which means 'Yahweh is gracious'), great, i.e. a prophet, a life-long Nazirite like Samuel, from the first under God's control, the bringer of reformation in an evil age, the fulfiller of Malachi's closing promise (4.5 f.) in its spiritual meaning ('in the spirit and power of Elijah'). It contained, however, an interesting change; 'the hearts of children to their fathers' becomes 'the disobedient to the wisdom of the just'. The generation gap has always existed, and it is the duty of parents, not to complain about it, but to try to understand and bridge it. On the other hand, when the children are touched by the Spirit of God, they must recognize that it is their godly parents who are correct.

Asking for a sign (18) may show faith or doubt; Zechariah doubted and so was punished. The people wondered at his delay, for entry into the Temple was considered dangerous and was kept as short as possible. They realized he had seen a vision, when he could give only the gestures of the Aaronic blessing but not the words.

2 : The Chosen Vessel

Luke 1.26–56

Of Mary's background we know nothing beyond the fact that she was descended from David. The universal Jewish custom of the time tells us that she was between twelve and twelve and a half when she was engaged, i.e. legally became Joseph's wife; she must have been under fourteen when Gabriel came to her, for that was the maximum age at which a marriage was consummated. Since Mary did not know that he was an angel, and it was bad form to speak to a strange woman, she was greatly troubled. Gabriel's message contains overtones of Isa. 7.14; 2 Sam. 7.14; Isa. 9.7; Dan. 7.14. Mary realized that this was not a promise about a child she might have by Joseph (34) but of one to be conceived almost immediately.

Gabriel told her this would be the work of the Holy Spirit (35). We would do well to be satisfied with this and not to seek for purely human explanations of the Virgin Birth and of the breaking of the entail of original sin. 'The child will be called holy' means he would belong entirely to God; 'Son of God' before Jesus' resurrection meant for a Jew the perfect revealer of God's character and will. In v. 37, 'for God's promises can never fail' (NEB, Phillips), is preferable. A godly Jewess did not need to be reminded of God's omnipotence; what was important for her was that the ancient promises were going into effect. 'I am the handmaid of the Lord' (38) means 'I am the Lord's slave'.

Mary's poem of thanksgiving should be compared with Hannah's (1 Sam. 2.1–10), on which it is obviously based. Both celebrated God's reversal of man's standards and values. A concept of Christianity that makes it a religion of the *status quo* has completely missed its nature, cf. 1 Cor. 1.26–31. Something of Mary's sweet humility is seen in her leaving

Elizabeth just before John's birth; she did not wish to deflect attention from her.

It is a great pity that the undue honour given Mary in certain circles, which has led to the attribution of sinlessness, a mediating role and worship, has caused others to give her too little. Though later Mary showed that she did not adequately understand the Son God had given her, yet in her humble acceptance of God's overwhelming will for her she is an object lesson for all.

3 : Joseph

Matthew 1.1–25 (Luke 3.23–38)

The main purpose of the genealogy is probably less to prove Jesus' legal claim to the Davidic throne, and more to show that He was not merely a revealer of divine truth but far more the climax of a divinely guided historical process. Luke gives His genealogy (3.23–38), which is also of Joseph, cf. NBD, p. 459, after the Baptism, so as to set Jesus' work as man in its human setting and to show Him as the second Adam. There can be little doubt that Jechoniah (Jehoiachin) in v. 11 is a scribal error for Johoiakim, which goes back to the Hebrew original. The device of breaking up the genealogy into three groups of fourteen names stresses the natural divisions of the history, gives an aid to memory, and stamps the name of David on each, for the value of the letters of his name in Hebrew adds up to fourteen.

Preferable in v. 18 is 'This is the story of the birth of the Messiah' (NEB, RSV mg.). Joseph is not called husband (19) in anticipation; their engagement made them a married couple —hence the need for a divorce, if they were to part. Joseph, by his acceptance of Mary and her child, made Jesus his legal son. Jesus (Heb. Yeshua) was the then accepted abbreviation of Joshua (Heb. *Yehoshua*) meaning Yahweh is Salvation, and was at the time a very common name. We constantly demand the new; God takes the old and fills it with a new meaning.

In Isa. 7.14 the RSV, NEB, Phillips, Knox, Jer.B. translate young woman or maiden, for the Hebrew word means an unmarried girl of marriageable age, whose virginity is taken for granted—hence the Greek, 'virgin', as quoted by Matthew. This prophecy, like numerous others, had a double fulfilment.

By the time a girl, on the eve of marriage when Isaiah spoke, bore her first child, the danger threatening Jerusalem would have apparently passed; thrilled by the fact, his parents would call him Immanuel. Isaiah's further words show that the deliverance would be only apparent, and that the reality would come only after judgement, cf. Isa. **7**.17; **9**.2; **11**.1. Even had he used the technical word for virgin, its full implications would have become apparent only in the fulfilment. Though Jesus was Immanuel in the full sense, this could be grasped and enjoyed fully only after He was experienced as Saviour, so Jesus was the name given Him.

4 : The Nativity

Luke 2.1–20

In re-reading this most familiar of stories we must make an effort to rid ourselves of the pagan and sentimental accretions of popular tradition. All Israel did not go off to the cities of their most distant ancestors; Joseph, as the legal heir to the Davidic throne (Matt. **1**.1–16), had for obvious reasons kept his legal domicile in Bethlehem. There is no suggestion that they went there in winter and still less that Jesus was born on the night they arrived; if anything, v. 6 means the exact opposite. The word rendered 'inn' (except NEB) is elsewhere (**22**.11; Mark **14**.14) a guest room and should be so understood here. Owing to its nearness to Jerusalem it is improbable that Bethlehem had an inn at the time. The manger means no more than the portable wooden trough used for feeding the animals when they were admitted to the lower level of a house. The ox and ass of earlier Christian art—now multiplied to a whole farmyard!—were taken from Isa. **1**. 3 and were intended merely as a symbolic linking with Old Testament prophecy. The 'swaddling clothes' (7, 12) stress the normality of the baby. While there may be poverty in the picture, it is not abnormal; such could have been the surroundings of most new-born babies in Palestine.

It is often stressed that the sheep pastured in the fields of Bethlehem were destined for Temple sacrifices, and therefore their shepherds were chosen for pious reputation. This is doubtless true but should not be stressed. Theophilus (**1**.3) could not have known this; had Luke laid any stress on it, he would have explained it. Rather, the revelation of David's 'greater Son' was given to those who followed David's profession. However beautiful and true the AV rendering of the song of the heavenly host (14), the manuscript evidence is overwhelmingly in favour of the RV, RSV, NEB; the last renders well, '. . .for men on whom His favour rests'.

The shepherds' story created wonder among those who heard it (18). 'Wonder'—this looks forward to the ultimate rejection of Christ. The union of heaven's glory and absolute human normality is something that men feel to be irreconcilable. So they either reject or distort the balance. The popular distortion of the Christmas story can be particularly disastrous in the effect it has on young children, as it makes it seem like a fairy story.

5 : Earliest Infancy

Luke 2.21–39

Today circumcision is regarded by the average Jew mainly as a national sign, and by many non-Jews as a hygienic measure, but in New Testament times it was above all an indication that the child was under an obligation to keep the Law, cf. Gal. 4.4; hence the question of Gentile Christians' keeping the Law could be summed up by the demand for their circumcision. Part of Jesus' obedience was His acceptance of the conditions under which He was born. In the rare cases where we find Him stepping outside these limitations, it was for the good of others, and He normally justified His action by an appeal to Scripture.

The RSV and NEB follow older manuscripts in v. 22 in contrast to the AV. The latter conforms to the language of Lev. 12.1–5. By saying 'their purification' Luke was expressing the obvious fact that if the mother needed purification so did the child. He is not implying that Jesus needed it; it is his way of expressing Paul's phrase, 'sending His own Son in the likeness of sinful flesh' (Rom. 8.3). It is in Christ's resurrection that we have the assurance of His perfect sinlessness and deity (Rom. 1.4).

Simeon's hymn is based throughout on Old Testament Scripture, especially Isaiah. For 'a light for revelation to the Gentiles', cf. Isa. 42.6; 49.6 and to some extent 60.3. Jesus is

14

Israel (Isa. **49**.3), and so its glory, for He is everything that Israel should have been and was not, that Israel wished to be and yet could not be. Jesus is the perfect revelation of God to the world and the perfect justification of God's election of Israel.

The only way in which v. 39 can reasonably be reconciled with the story in Matt. **2** is first of all to separate the latter from Luke's nativity story by a period of time, as is indeed suggested by Herod's killing of the boys up to two years of age. It may thus be understood that after the presentation in the Temple Joseph and Mary returned to Nazareth (39) and sold up there. Then they returned to Bethlehem. Joseph evidently considered that the promised Messiah should not only be born but also brought up in David's city. Luke had no interest in mentioning the second Bethlehem visit, for, unlike Matthew, he does not stress Jesus as the Messianic king but as the representative man, cf. his tracing of His genealogy back to Adam.

6 : The Coming of the Magi

Matthew 2.1–23

In this story too we must strip away modern sentimental accretions. We are not told how many astrologers (NEB, Phillips) there were—earlier Christian tradition suggested up to twelve—and they were certainly not kings. Presumably the rising of the star (NEB, Jer.B.) was at the time of Jesus' birth, so their arrival must have been at least some months later, cf. v. 16. There is no suggestion that they were led by the star, cf. v. 9. Matthew does not explain how the astrologers came to link the star with the expected king of the Jews —he does not even mention Num. **24**.17—what its nature was, or how it could at the last move before them. The important thing is that none of the priests and scribes (4) had the least interest in following up the matter; that was left to Gentiles, thus foreshadowing the ultimate outcome. The NEB and Phillips are very much better in vs. 2, 8, 11 with 'to pay him homage'. There is no suggestion that they recognized Jesus' deity.

'Gold, frankincense and myrrh' are very often expounded allegorically, but unless we assume that the astrologers had

15

been given a special revelation, it is hardly wise to attribute knowledge to them unshared by their Jewish contemporaries. Perhaps we should rather see God's providing: gold for the cost of the expensive journey to Egypt; frankincense and myrrh, easy to transport but very valuable in Egypt, where they were in great demand for embalming, and so covering costs until Joseph could find work.

When Matthew applied Hos. 11.1 (15) and Jer. 31.15 (17, 18) to Jesus, he was implying that He was the fulfilment and personification of Israel. In some way He had to recapitulate Israel's history, the hidden years in Nazareth paralleling the wilderness wanderings. Rachel's sorrow was due to sin and a foreign king. Now these were combined in a king (Herod) with no claim to the throne. In addition, Jer. 31.15 stands in close connection with the promise of the new covenant (Jer. 31.31–34). So, too, the fulfilment of the promise was ushered in by suffering. Nazareth (23) is not mentioned in the Old Testament, but Nazarene (*notzri*) is reminiscent of 'shoot' (*netzer*) in Isa. 11.1. In addition, the low status of Nazareth (John 1.46) corresponds to that of the Suffering Servant.

7 : The Boy Jesus

Luke 2.40–52

Luke, stressing Jesus' role as representative man, points out that His development was that of a normal child and adolescent (40, 52). The stress was needed, for perverse natural piety was to delight in portraying Him as 'wielding the power of the Godhead with a child's waywardness and petulance', to quote Salmon on the Gospel of St. Thomas, dating back in some form to about A.D. 200. We should never try to go behind the New Testament and infer what knowledge and powers Jesus possessed before He began His ministry.

A Jewish boy, then as now, reached his religious majority at thirteen. Normally one began to initiate him into his religious responsibilities a year earlier, which shows why Jesus was twelve, when first taken to Jerusalem (42). Public teaching in the Temple (46) took place only on Sabbaths and feast-days. The feast had not finished when Jesus was found, so we infer that because of poverty Joseph and Mary started their return journey on the third day of Passover, when travel was again permitted and the main obligations of the feast had been fulfilled. An important part in Rabbinic teaching was played by listeners' questions; normally these were answered by questions designed to draw out the answer from the questioner. Hence we have a picture, not of Jesus teaching the rabbis, but a Boy of twelve asking questions not expected from that age, and when questioned in return showing knowledge (in the context, of a religious nature) far beyond what was expected.

The AV and Jer.B. in v. 49 subtly suggest that Jesus had misunderstood His Father's will. In fact, He was telling Mary that there had been no need to search; it was obvious that He would be in the Temple. Possibly Mary had used the opportunity of this visit to reveal the secret of His birth to Him.

In v. 52 we have a reminiscence of 1 Sam. **2**.26; Prov. **3**.4. The wisdom is that which comes from experience, from which most are so unwilling to learn. One could easily build too much on 'in favour with God'. Ponder Heb. **2**.10, 18; **5**.7–9, for these passages will have had their main fulfilment in the years in Nazareth. Remember, too, that in spite of the modern cult of youth, it has little value except as a fore-shadowing of what maturity may bring.

Questions and themes for study and discussion on Studies 1-7

1. Is it ever right to ask for a sign? If so, when?
2. Compare and contrast the experience of Mary and Hannah.
3. Why are there so many genealogies in Scripture?
4. What makes men want to embroider the Nativity narrative and other Bible stories?
5. Why do you think Simeon was kept alive to see the Christ when others did not have this privilege?
6. In what ways can Jesus be described as 'the fulfilment and personification of Israel'?
7. What may modern parents learn from the story of our Lord's first Passover?

CHARACTER STUDIES

8 : Uzziah

2 Kings 15.1–7; 2 Chronicles 26

The greatest king of Judah since Solomon and David was known by two names. The meanings are not remotely different —Azariah means 'Yahweh-his-helper', and Uzziah, 'Yahweh-his-strength'. Uzziah may have changed his name, or it may have been changed on his accession.

He was a mere boy when he became king, but he set to work with all the drive and energy of youth to establish his borders. A modern Israeli, conscious of the strategic necessities of his country, would understand and applaud the measures of this energetic young ruler. He cleared the way to Israel's old southern outlet, the Gulf of Aqaba and the port of Elath. He subdued the Gaza strip, and the coastal plain where the Philistines still held a measure of their old strength. He penetrated the arid but strategically significant Negev, the desert of the Sinai Peninsula. He acquired power on his eastern borderlands, where the old Ammonite enemy threatened his rear. The situation is curiously prophetic of 1967.

Uzziah then made Jerusalem strong, built an arsenal of sophisticated weaponry, and trained an élite corps of soldiers. In this last act is a pointer to the thought and the ideal which dominated the young man's life. David had his band of 600 heroes, men of warlike valour who formed his bodyguard. Uzziah increased this regiment to 2,600. He quite clearly had David in mind. He wanted to be like his great predecessor. Hence his measures for his land's security, and his devotion.

A fine example, a model of excellence, can be a beneficent force in a life. The Christian does not want for one in his Lord, but such glory apart, he can often find one in a fellow Christian. We shall see this theme continue for a full half-century. ' Example,' said Burke, 'is the school of mankind. They will learn at no other.' Example is the first great gift we can bestow upon the world. 'Alexander,' Sir Philip Sidney once remarked, 'received more bravery of mind by the pattern of Achilles than by hearing the definition of fortitude.'

It was Goldsmith's parson who 'allured to better worlds and led the way'.

Such a force in Uzziah's life was David. He enjoyed half a century of distinguished royalty, and then through presumption contracted leprosy. Such tragedies occur. But Uzziah's influence, his salutary example, lived on. 'Of all commentaries on Scripture,' said John Donne, 'examples are the best and liveliest.'

9 : The Prophet

Isaiah 6; 32.1–8

Uzziah found an example, and in the process became one. There was a young man in his kingdom who was marked for greatness. 'In the year that King Uzziah died' the young nobleman had a vision of God which changed his life. There is surely no other interpretation of the phrase. The monarch, so royal, so able, so good, and in his end so tragic, had been a tremendous example, a shining influence, in another life. The shock of his sad ending was used of God to claim Isaiah for His own.

Isaiah probably had his hero in mind when he wrote his thirty-second chapter with its image of the rock in the wilderness. 'Where the desert touches an oasis,' wrote Sir George Adam Smith, Palestine's great geographer, 'life is continually under attack from the wind-driven sand. The rains come, and a carpet of green struggles to life on the desert's edge and there is promise of fertility. But it is doomed, for the thirsting sand creeps in, and stunts and chokes the aspirations of the green. But set a rock in the sand. After brief rains, life springs up on the leeward side and in time becomes a garden. The boulder has stayed the drift.'

So a man can stand in the wind's way, endure the harsh sand-laden blast of the hot khamsin, and protect from withering death the weaker life that finds refuge behind its protecting body. It is a noble function for any man thus to face the death-bearing wind and the beating of the storm. That is what our Lord did on Calvary. We do not know the details, but such could have been the role Uzziah played in the young Isaiah's life. According to Jewish tradition, Isaiah was of royal blood, and it may be inferred from his own writings that

19

he was of high social station. Such situations have their peculiar temptations, and one like the king could have been a 'shelter in a weary land' to a beleaguered and bewildered boy, hard-pressed in his court and entourage.

To stand like a rock and preserve feebler life is an exacting task. If Uzziah saw his young relative grow to vigour under his shade, it was rich reward. And such worth propagates itself. Isaiah became such a defence to Hezekiah. God is creative and goes on.

10 : Ahaz

2 Kings 16; Isaiah 1

Jotham's undistinguished reign probably overlapped with that of Uzziah. It is not clear for how long the good king, whom Isaiah so admired, was incapacitated by his dread disease, and unable to perform the duties of royalty. It may be guessed that some years of Jotham's reign were devoted to a regency. And he died at the age of forty-one.

No lineaments of his character emerge from the narrative which seems to grow condensed and hurried as it moves on to final catastrophe. Then came Ahaz, at the age of twenty, to the throne. Isaiah exercised his ministry from Uzziah on to Hezekiah, and the beginnings of his major activity must have taken place in the reigns of Jotham and Ahaz.

Over neither king had Isaiah the influence which he held in his maturer years, and to such effect, over Hezekiah. Ahaz went his way, and in the record of the Book of Kings the military disaster which accompanied his activities is apparent. Israel's southern outlet at Elath on the Gulf of Aqaba was lost to a Syrian counter-attack. Uzziah's work in establishing the borders was undone.

Then in his crass folly the baffled king sought to call in the aid of the sinister power of Assyria against the old Syrian foe. He successfully bribed Tiglath-pileser with the sacred treasures of the land, who needed small inducement to move murderously south. It was a grim development.

The action showed the folly of Ahaz' mind and the poverty of his spirit. The people had, as peoples so often do have, the ruler they deserved. The first five chapters of Isaiah are probably chronologically previous to the sixth, and the indictment of a corrupt and backslidden community contained in the opening chapters of that most eloquent book of prophecy reveal the declension of Judah. It was a state of affairs against which Isaiah bravely and passionately protested. In him Uzziah's heritage continued. Ahaz stumbled on with his pagan altar (**16**.10) to an early death at the age of thirty-six. Wisely, Isaiah had concentrated on his son. A generation is sometimes to be written off. It need not be an older group. Ahaz' folly lay between the years of twenty and thirty-six. Find time to read the opening chapters of Isaiah.

11 : The Prophet Again

Isaiah 7; 9.1–7

In the pattern of human life God requires no more than a man's surrender to His will. Anything abandoned to His use can win significance untold, meaning and creative influence beyond and above surrounding circumstance, and worth unimagined by the one who surrenders the poor scrap of human raw material to God's hand.

There was a fool on the throne of Judah, a man whom the strongest and bravest voice in his kingdom was unable to influence. Isaiah might have accounted his work vain and his efforts wasted with the weakling Ahaz. He was probably not aware that, in looking beyond him, and yearning in eloquent poetry for a ruler of God's anointing, he was catching a vision of the King of kings.

Isaiah's rich writing is not always easy reading, but the mind of a great poet, a leader of surpassing worth and courage, and a man of God of deepest insight, comes through to the reader. We feel that we know Isaiah and see him in his visions.

In chapters **7** and **9** he did not know that he was writing words which a future century was to invest with shining truth. He was merely committed and surrendered to the Eternal One, ready to do the task before him, and in such fellowship spoke beyond his time and place. 'The Messianic prophecies of the Old Testament,' wrote Sir George Adam Smith, ' are tidal rivers. They not only run to the sea, which is Christ; they feel His reflex influence. It is not enough for the Christian to have followed the historical direction of the

prophecies, or to have proved their connection with the New Testament as parts of one Divine Harmony. Forced back by the fullness of meaning to which he has found their courses open, he returns to find the savour of the New Testament upon them, and that where he descended shallow and tortuous channels, with all the difficulties of historical exploration, he is borne back on full tides of worship . . . "the Lord is with him there, a place of broad rivers and streams" (Isa. 33.21).'
What a man was the vehicle of such unveiling!

Questions and themes for study and discussion on Studies 8-11

1. Example cuts both ways.
2. Consider the image of the Rock in Scripture.
3. Compare and contrast the characters of Uzziah and Ahaz.
4. How do we justify reading the Old Testament in the light of the New?

THE LIFE OF CHRIST

The Opening of Jesus' Ministry

12 : John's Ministry

Luke 3.1–20 (Matt. 3.1–12; Mark 1.1–8; John 1.19–28)

In popular thought little place is found for John's ministry in spite of a statement like Luke 7.24–28. Jesus is pictured as sweeping at least the common people off their feet by His eloquence and love, the simplicity of His teaching and His miracles. In at least four features John was responsible for an all-important preparation.

1. John was a 'freak', Jesus was a normal man (Luke 7.33 f). Repeatedly the abnormal man standing on the fringe of society has been needed to stir the conscience and imagination of those tied to routine before another could change society from within. The best Old Testament example is Elijah and his successor Elisha. To go out into the wilderness is not normally God's way of salvation, but until some do the masses will not be stirred to seek the narrow gate that leads to life (Matt. 7.13 f).

2. At the time there was a deep and burning hope of the Messianic deliverer, cf. Luke 2.25, 38; John 1.19–21, but it was, as is the Second Coming today, all too often a subject of discussion and speculation. John brought it to focus and made it a reality. We must not forget that what led His contemporaries to accept or reject Jesus was normally their decision whether He was or was not one whom they could accept as Messiah.

3. Though it was generally accepted that the Messiah's coming was linked with religious and moral demands, these were generally taken to be superficial and marginal. We see some of them reflected in the New Testament purity of race (8), observance of the ritual law, cf. the Sabbath controversies, fasting (Mark 2.18–22), ritual washing (Mark 7.1–8). The Zealots, fanatical nationalists, considered national liberation justified murder and other illegal acts; some preached what today is called a Socialist revolution. John stressed that the coming of the Kingdom of God (Matt. 3.2) meant judge-

ment as well as blessing, the criterion being life not words.

4. At least two of Jesus' first disciples (John 1.35) were first among John's, and John 1.35–51 probably implies that all mentioned there had been first influenced by him.

It is important to remember that though John had withdrawn from society (Luke 1.80), his demands were all to be carried out within society. Much of his teaching is reflected in 1 Cor 7.24. Note that his 'socialism' (11) was based on giving, not taking. His baptism implied a completely new beginning.

13 : The Baptism and Temptation

Luke 3.21, 22; 4.1–13 (Matt. 3.13–4.11; Mark 1.9–13; John 1.24–34)

Though John and Jesus were cousins (Luke 1.36), it is unlikely there had been many contacts. So John's unwillingness to baptize Him was probably due to prophetic insight rather than personal knowledge. Jesus' willingness to be baptized was part of His identification with sinners. In addition, as said on Luke 2.22 (Study No. 5), it is the resurrection which is the Father's guarantee of His Son's sinlessness. In all four accounts the stress is on the descent of the Holy Spirit. We are to theorize on what it meant for God to face human difficulties and temptations. In the Gospels the stress is that Jesus was the perfect Man, who from His conception (Luke 1.35) was kept holy by the Spirit, who also caused Him to triumph in temptation. We are asked to share in that power.

The Father's commendation (22) was, as the Greek makes clear, not merely His approval of the Baptism, but also and primarily His acceptance of His life up till then. Through the Septuagint it is also linked with Isa. 42.1.

It would be truer to the meaning of the Greek and the spiritual significance of the story, if we spoke of testing rather than temptation, the older meaning of which was testing. Jesus was not being urged to do anything morally wrong, but simply to follow entirely natural impulses without reference to the Spirit's guidance. The first was to use spiritual powers for personal ends (3). Jesus used these powers to feed or heal, when the needs of others demanded it, but never as an advertisement. The quotation from Deut. 8.3b implies that

God, the Giver of all, should decide how His gifts should be used. The second (5–7) was a call to compromise in recognition of the fact that Satan is the ruler of this world (John **14**.30; 1 John **5**.19). The NEB renders better with 'do homage'. But the recognition of other powers in this way is a denial of God's omnipotence. The third (9–11) suggested that God be forced to display His miraculous powers on His behalf. We fall into this temptation easily, thinking we glorify God by forcing Him to show His power. The power is there, but it must be used as God wishes. Matthew transposes the second and third, probably because he is stressing Jesus' role as King.

14 : The First Disciples

John 1.29–51

John said of Jesus. 'He must increase, but I must decrease' (John **3**.30) and allowed his conviction above all by passing on his disciples to Jesus (35–37). Though unprovable, it is probable that all six mentioned here had been influenced by John first. 'He first' (41) probably implies that the unnamed disciple, i.e. John, then found his brother James. Nathanael, cf. **21**.2, is probably Bartholomew, who is always paired with Philip in the Synoptic lists (Matt. **10**.3; Mark **3**.18; Luke **6**.14). Andrew's and Philip's words (41, 45) show that both Peter and Nathanael were deeply concerned with the coming Messiah promised by John. Our tendency is to press the younger Christian to committal in Christian work. Jesus permitted these six, and perhaps the others also, to get to know Him more closely before He called them to complete identification with Him, cf. Mark **1**.16–20. After all, the Spirit knows the right time better than we do.

It is clear that the whole section from v. 19 on comes after Jesus' temptation. It was given to John to see, even though he could hardly have known the details—these were probably given to the disciples after the resurrection—that Jesus by His rejection of Satan's suggestions had made the pathway of suffering and death inevitable, and hence was the Servant of Isa **53**. The AV and RV are correct in placing 'beareth' in the margin (29) alongside 'taketh away'; both are implied, cf. RSV mg. to 1 Pet. **2**.24.

We have here an array of titles given to Jesus: Lamb of God (29), Son of God (34, 49)—for the usage see comments on Luke 1.35—Rabbi (38,49), i.e. Teacher, Messiah (41), King of Israel (49), yet clearly they come to a climax in Son of Man, the representative man and the coming world ruler (Dan. 7.13). It is often stated that John, in contrast to the Synoptics, stresses the deity rather than the manhood of Jesus. In fact, all these titles are illuminated in various ways in this Gospel, but above all, the last, even though it is not used so often. The mystery John illumines is above all how God can be truly man. It is this mystery that creates the ladder linking God and man (51). It is not likely that we should lay any special stress on the angels. Jesus is the one and only true link by which man's needs ascend to God and God's blessings descend to man. The angels may bear the gifts but they are Jesus' servants, and through Him ours (Heb. 1.14).

15 : The First Miracle

John 2.1–12

John records seven miracles by Jesus and uses the term ' sign ' to designate them, though he indicates that there were many more (20.30). The limitation to seven and the use of 'sign' indicate that the stories chosen have a deeper purpose than the mere narration of the miraculous.

Certain details can easily be added to John's account. Mary's active participation behind the scenes suggests that one of the bridal pair was a relation. Possibly, Jesus and His disciples were invited at the last moment; this would explain the wine's running short and Mary's turning to Jesus; there is no evidence that she expected a miracle. Jesus' answer defies idiomatic translation. She is ' woman ', cf. 19.26, not ' Mother', for His actions were not to be swayed by special affection to her or the bridal couple. Then her approach to the problem was not His. He knew the need, but awaited His hour (4), i.e. the time appointed by the Father for Him to work, cf. 7.3-10. It may be that having filled the six jars with water, the servants then drew more from the well (Westcott), or that only what was taken from the jars became wine (NBC); John's failure to make this clear shows how unimportant it was to him.

The various attempts at symbolic or allegoric interpretation have nothing to commend them. It is clear from v. 11 that John is writing of something that had an immediate effect on the disciples, not of deeper meanings which gradually came to them.

Temple may well be correct in seeing a picture of the change brought about by our first contact with Christ, 'a change like that from water to wine'. The coming of Christ may well bring distortions and needs to our lives. There is many a hard-pressed family which wonders how it can possibly meet the demands of Christ's work at home and abroad, demands on time as well as money, if it opens itself to His demands. Yet if He is welcomed—it may be at the moment when all human resources run out—from what is there Christ can provide the extra that is needed, an extra bringing joy in its train. What Jesus would not do for Himself in the wilderness He now did for those who had invited Him to share their joy. As for Himself, He foreshadowed the future by leaving home (12).

Questions and themes for study and discussion on Studies 12-15

1. John the Baptist has been called 'the neglected prophet'. Can you suggest reasons for this neglect?
2. It has been said that just as the cross and the resurrection throw light on each other, so also do our Lord's baptism and temptations. In what ways?
3. What was there about Jesus which was so attractive to the men who left all to follow Him?
4. How do we see the glory of Christ manifested in His first miracle?

CHARACTER STUDIES

16 : Hezekiah the Reformer

2 Chronicles 29; 2 Kings 18.1–12

King Hezekiah was twenty-five years of age when he came to
Judah's throne, and his reign of almost thirty years was one
of the finest of all Jerusalem's kings. Under Ahaz the land
had gone astray. The old strong, stern religion which had
ennobled Jewish life had decayed before those exotic cults
which demanded less in clean and upright living, and made
rituals of carnality and vice. It is part of an evil bent in man
to welcome release from discipline. There is always welcome
in contaminated corners of society for leave to relax a moral
bond.

So, in the ancient story, it came to pass that Jerusalem's
Temple stood abandoned. Rubbish and dirt filled the holy
place. The shrine which Solomon had built was no grand,
imposing edifice, but it was a beautiful little place, lavishly
adorned. The holy vessels were gone, turned into cash by the
dead king, but the building itself remained, dishonoured and
neglected, the sign and symbol of the state of old tradition
and the nation's soul.

The young king lost no time in parley or diplomacy. Youthful, ardent, loyal, he saw no impediments, and scorned delay
in doing what he knew was right. In the first month of his
reign he cleansed the Temple. He called upon the Levites to
begin the task by a cleansing of their own lives (2 Chron.
29.5), and having met this prime condition for all of God's
work, to turn their hands to the task before them. The young
man, prompted perhaps by Isaiah, showed deep spiritual
insight. Youth often does.

It took the Levites a full week to remove the uncleanness
from a building no larger than the average city church. No
one had seen the rubble and the rubbish carried in. Evil
accumulates unseen in the temple of the life (2 Cor. **6**.16).
The small surrenders, the petty sins, the casual indulgences,
the little disloyalties, accumulate unnoticed, until the holy
place within becomes a house of shame. Said Masefield:

> *My soul has many an old decaying room*
> *Hung with the ragged arras of the past . . .*

28

We must rend such things apart and let God's sunshine in.

Here, then, was a young man giving to God the rich enthusiasm of his young manhood. God can use such gifts. Hezekiah breaks into the pages of Scripture like a refreshing breeze. He had grown up in 'the shadow of a Rock'. The cleansing of the Temple was a symbolic act which Jerusalem well understood. Under the young king's dynamic leadership the people returned to their ancient ways and pure religion.

17 : Sennacherib (1)

Isaiah 8 and 10

As though to mock such wholehearted reformation, the new king of Assyria moved south. The bandit kings of that brutal empire have left a name of horror. Says one of them: 'To the city of Tela I approached. The inhabitants would not come down and embrace my feet. With battle and slaughter I captured the city. Three thousand of their fighting men I slew. Many I burned. I cut off the hands and feet of some. I built a pyramid of living captives and a pyramid of heads. Their young men and their maidens I burned with fire'. The imagination reels at the monster's cruelty. And he gloried in the deed and carved it on his palace wall.

Such vile words could be paralleled again and again.

But mark the faith which dared to throw defiance at such a force. Isaiah pictures the gloating of the grim invader, and brands him for an arrogant fool who boasts of evil and fails to see that he is no more than God's axe, a tool in His hand, permitted for a season to wreak ill (10.5, 15).

They were tense and evil days. The vivid passage of dramatic poetry which closes ch. 10 pictures the invasion rolling south. They were days which this century knows too well. The smoke of burning villages shows darker in the north. The panting messengers come in, and name after name appears on the war-maps (28–32). At Michmash, where Jonathan with one brave helper had once done wonders, the Assyrian might perhaps have been held. He swept resistance out of the pass (28, 29).

Jerusalem went frantically to work. There was no water in the city, and Hezekiah's engineers took up the task of bringing the waters of the Virgin's Spring into the Pool of Siloam.

In 1880, two Arab schoolboys playing in the tunnel, found an ancient inscription. The moss was cleaned away, and scholars read: 'This is how the sap was cut. When the workers were lifting up their picks each towards his fellow (the tunnel was cut from both ends), and when there were yet three cubits to be cut, heard was the voice of each calling to his fellow. And they struck each to meet his fellow pick against pick.' There is something appropriate in the fact that the only inscription from Jerusalem which we can set against Sennacherib's proud boasts is the simple story of a band of navvies carved on a culvert wall. On the valour of simple men dictators break.

18 : Sennacherib (2)

2 Chronicles 32

Meanwhile Sennacherib was storming Lachish, a day's journey away. And here Hezekiah's heart failed him and he sent tribute. Appeasement will not work with ravening wolves. Sennacherib took the tribute and demanded surrender. Isaiah encouraged the king, and he returned a defiant answer. The die was cast, and these were the days when the city hung on the prophet's words. The king left a division to watch Jerusalem, and swung south to finish Egypt.

At Pelusium one of the strangest disasters in history happened. There was nothing strange in it, however, to the Hebrew historians. 'The angel of the Lord,' said they in boldness of faith, 'went forth and slew a hundred and eighty-five thousand in the camp of the Assyrians' (2 Kings **19**.35). There is a magnificent piece of poetry in Isaiah which probably dates from this day. 'Ah, the booming of many peoples which boom like the booming of the seas, and the rushing of nations that make a rushing like the rushing of many waters. The nations shall rush like the rushing of many waters, but He checketh it, and they shall flee afar off, and shall be chased as the chaff of the mountains before the wind, and like the whirling dust before the storm. At eventide behold terror, and before the morning they are not' (George Adam Smith's translation of **17**.12–14).

Herodotus, the Greek historian, tells a story of the same event. He heard it in Egypt. The statue which the Egyptians set up to commemorate their deliverance held a mouse, the symbol of pestilence, in its hand. Mice and rats communicate bubonic plague, and pour into the homes of men when smitten with the disease. Was it bubonic plague which 'breathed on the face of the host as it passed'?

The broken remnant struggled home to Assyria, and Sennacherib never came again, although it was twenty years before he died on the swords of his sons.

Byron wrote of the Assyrian disaster:

> The Assyrian came down like a wolf on the fold,
> And his cohorts were gleaming in purple and gold;
> And the sheen of his spears was like stars on the sea,
> Where the blue wave rolls nightly on deep Galilee.
> Like the leaves of the forest when summer was green,
> That host with its banners at sunset was seen.
> Like the leaves of the forest when autumn is blown,
> That host on the morrow lay withered and strown.

Like some ancient Churchill, in a day of stress, Isaiah had held his people's strength against all odds.

19 : Isaiah's Secret

Isaiah 30.1–15; 32.1–17

Someone once built a verse out of words and phrases from Isaiah:

> In quietness and confidence
> Shall be my strength each day,
> The Lord will go before me to straighten all the way.
> So I'll walk with an assurance,
> Nor fear the darkest hour,
> For God will there reveal to me His glory and His power.

Over the last few studies we have looked at the tumultuous days of the great Assyrian attack. Isaiah can be understood only in the dark context of such times. They were tense and testing days of the sort which bring out the best and the worst in the spirit of man. Set the calm confident man of God over against the panic-stricken populace, as the peril rolled south.

We see Isaiah move with fearless dignity through the chaos of his day, firm in his quiet faith, sure in his God. The two last verses in the passages prescribed above give the reason, Isaiah's open secret of success. Strength flows from quiet trust, and both quietness and trust are the fruits of righteousness. It is obvious enough. There can be no peace if the heart is divided, housing the disloyalty of sin. Every man needs some island of peace within his person, some place of salutary tranquillity and withdrawal. God alone can provide such a retreat, as Isaiah most steadfastly maintains (**4**.6; **16**.4; **17**.10; **25**.4). All else will betray us in the pressure of disaster (**28**.15–17).

To this safe abiding place we must constantly retreat, to refresh and strengthen the spirit. It was Elijah's lack that, in the earthquake, the gale and the fire of his passionate life he had somewhere neglected this, and God's therapy was precisely in this area of his life. In 'returning and rest' is our daily salvation from stress, tension, the wear and tear of living, and all else that scars the mind and daunts the soul. 'Thou wilt keep him in peace, *peace,* whose mind is stayed on thee," runs **26**.3. The repetition is Hebrew's device of emphasis—and how happy!

20 : The Servant

Isaiah 52.13–53.12

We must turn, before leaving Isaiah, to a figure which dominates the second part of his book—from ch. **40** onwards. These chapters could be the work of the prophet's later years. There is no reason at all to suppose that they are the work of another man, or a second prophet of the same name. A theory first propounded by Bernhard Duhm, in 1892, maintained that there were no fewer than three Isaiahs, conflated and fused in the first century. The notion is typical of the wild conjectures which, in biblical studies, so often pass for serious and reasoned literary criticism. This is not the place to argue the case, but one monumental fact may be appropriately mentioned. In the Shrine of the Scrolls in Jerusalem is a magnificent copy of Isaiah, dated from the second century before Christ. There is no division between chapters **39** and **40**. The rabbis of over 2,000 years ago obviously knew nothing of the guess of Bernhard Duhm. It is for the reader to decide whether the modern critic is correct, or whether the scholars who lived four centuries after Isaiah were in possession of the true tradition. Tradition, in all criticism, is not to be lightly disregarded.

These chapters should be read with reverence. A Suffering Servant moves through their pages. Isaiah may have woven into his poetry the pain of personal experience, his own grief at rejection, his own vindication. He may, as the rabbis have maintained, have had suffering Israel in mind. But whatever be the occasion of composition, it is clear that the prophet, overwhelmed and overshadowed of God, was describing a Person beyond and above any sort of earthly model. The New Testament applies the so-called 'Servant-Songs' (**42**.1 ff.; **49**.1 ff.; **50**.4 ff.; **52**.13—**53**.12, and probably **61**.1 ff.) to the Lord, and it is clear, as the prophecy moves on, that a single figure has emerged, clearly visible down a vista of time, who is none other than Christ. It is a clear preview of the New Testament which Isaiah was granted. To these chapters the reader should return, reverently, questingly He is, like Isaiah, whom we now leave with his visions of glory, in the presence of his Saviour and his Lord. And consider the privilege granted a man who lived close to God to see with God's eyes, to be lifted from time, and share in the eternal.

Questions and themes for study and discussion on Studies 16-20

1. Trace the chain of Messianic prophecy previous to Isaiah.
2. Why must righteousness underlie peace?
3. Quote Christ and Paul on peace.
4. There are twenty references in the New Testament to the Servant Songs. List a dozen.

THE LIFE OF CHRIST

The Early Judean Ministry

21 : The Cleansing of the Temple

John 2.13–22

Sacrificial animals had to pass the scrutiny of the sacrificing priest. Hence, even for those living near Jerusalem, there was a major advantage in having a market of guaranteed animals; for those from other countries it was a necessity. Such a market was held on the Mount of Olives. It is easy to understand that the temple-authorities saw the advantage of having it held more under their control. The court of the Gentiles was not officially part of the Temple, though regarded as having a greater degree of sanctity than the rest of Jerusalem.

There is little difference between the story of the cleansing of the Temple and that in Mark 11.15–17, and it is widely maintained that there has been a misplacement, deliberate or accidental. The arguments used carry little conviction. The use of the court of the Gentiles as a cattle-market had such obvious advantages for the leading priests that a repetition was to be expected.

Jesus began His ministry by facing official Judaism in its citadel—note 'the Passover of the Jews' (13). In contrast to His second cleansing of the Temple, Jesus had come to Jerusalem as an unknown man, but by His actions and words ('My Father's house') He proclaimed His authority. He was asked to justify His claim (18), as He was more than once later, cf. Matt. 12.38; 16.1, because Moses had validated his mission by signs (Exod. 4.1–9, 30). Had Jesus refused any sign, we could understand it, but a purely future one (19), cf. Matt. 12.39, seems strange, until we remember that Moses had been given a future event as a sign (Exod. 3.12). To an enslaved people, ground down by hard labour, God might graciously give signs of His favour and presence, but where men claim to know Him, cf. John 8.33; 9.40 f., God's signs must be linked with the exercise of faith and come as a confirmation of it—but see the next section.

There was an ambiguity in the sign which Jesus' disciples

34

grasped only later (22). Because He was the true Temple, uniquely indwelt by the Holy Spirit (John 3.34), He was implicitly the One who would abolish this and any other earthly temple made with hands, cf. John 4.21; 1 Cor. 3.16; 6.19; Eph. 2.20–22; Rev. 21.22. Jesus had not yet begun His normal ministry. He was presenting Himself to the religious leaders of the people for recognition, but there was 'no beauty that they should desire him'.

22 : Nicodemus

John 2.23–3.21

We do not know the signs Jesus did in Jerusalem (23)—presumably compassionate acts of healing—but they were not intended as answers to the challenge in v. 18. For lovers of the miraculous there comes the staggering statement that though ' many trusted on his name . . . Jesus did not trust himself to them' (23 f., Temple)—a play on words normally ignored. The sight of the miraculous may produce a counterfeit of true faith that deceives all but Christ.

Nicodemus came representing his fellow teachers—'we' (2) —'by night', the most suitable time for serious conversation. His opening words were a politely veiled invitation for a specimen of Jesus' teaching; they wanted to know whether they could invite Him to join them in teaching. Compliments may make life easier, but they are out of place where the issues of life and eternity are involved. Further, the greater a person's religious knowledge the less the value of generalized discussion. By mentioning the Kingdom of God Jesus turned Nicodemus' attention to John's preaching (Matt. 3.1f); he may well have been one of the delegation of John 1.19–24. So water (5) probably refers to John's baptism, or rather the repentance with which it was linked; the suggestion that it stands for Christian baptism or the Scriptures has nothing to commend it. Jesus' surprise (10) was because the mention of water and spirit should have reminded Nicodemus of Ezek. 36.25–27. From vs. 11 f. we may infer that some of Jesus' disciples were present ('we') and also some of Nicodemus' ('you', plural), and such would have been normal Jewish practice. They had not understood or believed what Jesus had told them about things that happened 'on earth'

35

(12, NEB), hence it was pointless for Him to speak about the heavenly realities behind them. He could, for He had descended from heaven to be lifted up for man's salvation (13–15, cf. **12**.32). Jesus' use of 'Son of man' here (13) clearly refers to Dan. **7**.13. It is disputed whether 'who is in heaven' should be added to v. 13; if we do, it probably means 'whose home is in heaven' (NEB).

It is also disputed whether vs. 16–21 were said to Nicodemus (Phillips, NEB), or are a commentary by John (RSV). It is not important, for in either case they bring out the implications of vs. 14 f. Not all are covered by v. 18; some have had no possibility of belief because they have never heard. Perhaps we should say of them only that Christ died for them and in the judgement day will declare whether they would have believed had the possibility existed.

23 : The Forerunner Decreases

John 3.22–36

It may be that v. 24 merely corrects a false impression that could be created by Matt. **4**.12; Mark **1**.14; more probably it explains why Jesus' disciples, not Jesus, were baptizing (22, 26; **4**.1 f.). While His forerunner was still active, Jesus, though presenting Himself as the fulfiller of John's message, did nothing to detract from his activity. We saw that Jesus' first disciples had been linked with John; now they were continuing his work. This was not Christian baptism in the full sense.

It is immaterial whether we read 'a Jew' (RSV) or 'Jews' (AV, NEB) in v. 25. It seems that some tried to depreciate John's work by pointing to Jesus' greater popularity. The very fact that they disputed about purifying shows that the real points at issue had been forgotten or misunderstood. Standard Judaism was dominated by concepts of defilement and purification. This is no longer true, the destruction of the Temple —where purification was effected—having removed the possibility of it. They could not understand Christ's teaching on heart defilement (Mark **7**.1–23). Seeing defilement as something purely external, they could not understand the symbolism of John's baptism, not cleansing but a cutting off from the past, cf. 1 Pet. **3**.21 f.

It is difficult to say whether John fully realized what his

decreasing (30) involved. He had become so well known and popular that no slow elimination would have been adequate. His arrest by Herod and subsequent execution were a necessity and a measure of his greatness. We may be sure that John accepted this drastic decreasing without hesitation.

As with John 3.16–21, we cannot be sure whether we hear the evangelist's comments in vs. 31–36 or the voice of John the Baptist; the latter is more probable. In either case it explains why even the teaching ministry of John was inadequate compared to Jesus'. Some have taken 'yet no one receives his testimony' (32) as the evangelist's comment on the world situation at the time he wrote; this is improbable. We see from v. 32 that the statement should not be taken absolutely; rather it reinforces vs. 3, 5. Only the regenerate can really accept Jesus' teaching. 'It is not by measure that he gives the Spirit' (34) is a most important statement. On the basis of Phil. 2.7—'He emptied himself'—many claim that Jesus was ignorant of much and so liable to err. Though we know nothing precise of what the self-emptying involved, the Spirit 'without measure' is a guarantee of Jesus' infallibility.

24 : The Samaritan Woman

John 4.1–42

Having presented Himself to the leaders of Jewry, Jesus then did the same to the schismatic Samaritans. They were essentially the descendants of Ephraim and western Manasseh, with an admixture of foreign blood. Fundamentally orthodox, their chief aberrations were the rejection of all Old Testament books except the Pentateuch, and of Zion as God's choice for worship, claiming Mt. Gerizim (20) instead. Since their leaders were religiously illegitimate Jesus presented Himself obliquely through a woman—one of little repute at that. It is highly probable that Philip's successful ministry (Acts 8.5–8) in a city of Samaria (RSV, NEB, Jer.B.) was the sequel to what we read here.

Westcott points out that the verb translated 'left' (3) really means to leave something to itself. The report that Jesus was making more disciples than John (1) merely placed Him on the same general level and showed that the spiritual leaders had not recognized His true role. The only physical compulsion to pass through Samaria (4) was pressure of time and this seems denied by v. 40; hence it was more likely to be spiritual.

The woman, like many others, tried to hide her inner dissatisfaction by stress on non-essentials. It was less the sin and more the emptiness in her life that had been touched by Jesus. True, she tried to dodge the issue by raising the principal point of controversy between Jew and Samaritan (20), but, as with Thomas after the resurrection (John 20.24 f.), it was probably because she felt the possibility being held out to her too good to be true.

In a day when it is being increasingly suggested that the man in the street cannot grasp Christian theology it is worth stressing that Jesus expected this woman to understand a principle of God's nature, and hence of worship, which many theologians have failed to grasp. God, being spirit, does not need the material, however much He may use it for man's benefit (23 f).

We must beware of a Docetic Christ, i.e. one where manhood and its needs were merely an outward appearance. Just as He was genuinely hungry after His fast (Luke 4.2), so He was genuinely tired after a long tramp (6). The joy, however, of doing His Father's work (34) removed the natural pangs of hunger (32).

Questions and themes for study and discussion on Studies 21-24

1. What implications for Christian worship are there in the fact that our Lord is Himself the true Temple of God?
2. To what extent may the Christian come to share his Lord's discernment of what is in men?
3. Why did Jesus need a forerunner?
4. What can the Christian personal worker learn from the stories of Nicodemus and the Samaritan woman?

CHARACTER STUDIES

25 : Micah

Micah 6 and 7

Moresheth (1.1) was a settlement in the sheep hills which run like a spine down the length of Palestine, and this country village was the place of Micah's birth. We are looking for a man, not studying a book, so there is no great necessity to decide whether Micah's ministry ended with the reign of Hezekiah, or extended into the bad days which followed. It seems best to suppose that Micah did, indeed, live a long life, and uttered his last oracles under the evil rule of Manasseh. Hence chapters **6** and **7** for today's reading.

Moresheth is seventeen miles from Tekoa where Amos lived, and looks in the opposite direction. It is a thousand feet above the coastal plain, and fertile with the moisture of the Mediterranean winds. It bred no brooding children of the wilderness, but hard-working yeomen, aware of the surges of war on the plains beneath, but somewhat hidden by their hills and upland pastures, and simple in their rural detachment from the corruptions of the city. Famous scenes of Israel's history were in view . . . Lachish, Ekron, Ashdod and Gaza. Behind lay the hills of David's exile, the field of the fight with Goliath, the Adullam cave. It was a place to beget and to shape 'an Israelite indeed'. Catch the echoes in the text of Micah.

The prophecies of Amos and Hosea had been fulfilled upon the Northern Kingdom, and now, feeling the growing corruption of Jerusalem, and sensing the new perils of invasion, Micah uttered his prophecies. Whether these preceded Sennacherib, or whether they looked to ultimate destruction, need not detain us. The man's religion shows the man, and he stands in full portraiture in his small book, simple, ardent, devout.

He loathed social wrong and felt with passion for the poor (7.2 f.). He detested the hireling prophets whom Amos and Hosea had denounced (3.5ff). From such pain and involvement there arises in Micah's devoted mind the vision of hope, of a Zion yet to be, of a King yet to come. 'The

Blessed Hope' is never more needed than in such days, and it was Micah's honour to focus Israel's hope, perhaps with Isaiah's clarity, on the Great Redeemer (7.7). To this the theme passes to the climax, the warning, the prayer and the doxology, which close the book. Meditate in closing on 4.1, 2; 5.2; 7.8, 18. Here was a great and good man, who, in a few words, opened vistas of eternity.

26 : Manasseh's Evil

2 Kings 21.1–16

Manasseh reigned fifty-five years, longer than any other king of Judah, and it was a grim and sanguinary reign. Judah was helpless before the power of Assyria, and was tolerated while she kept the peace. As the New Testament shows, times of subjection and even occupation can know religious revival. John led his great wilderness ministry, and the Church was founded, during the Roman domination of Palestine. At the same time Christ was crucified, and the priestly castes turned the religion of the land into a barren ritual and a persecuting force.

In Manasseh's reign, the voice of prophecy, as the account shows, was not silent, but evil, centred in the court, and grounded in the character of the king, was paramount. Coming after the days of Hezekiah's revival, it was such a time as England saw when Charles II's court unwound the ways of Puritanism. Macaulay writes: 'Then came days never to be recalled without a blush, the days of servitude without loyalty, of sensuality without love, of dwarfish talents and gigantic vices, the paradise of cold hearts and narrow minds, the golden age of the coward, the bigot, and the slave.'

A weight of evil influence surrounded the boy king during the period of his regency. Isaiah, in spite of legends regarding his martyrdom under Manasseh, was probably dead, and Isaiah's closing visions of a prince of peace, and an age of God's benediction, were misunderstood, no doubt, and made the theme of disillusionment. Judah was little more than a vassal state. Obsequious courtiers, all through Israel's history, were notoriously evil counsellors. The gods and cults of the conqueror were measured by the conqueror's strength, and all through the Middle East, at this time, Assyria was the conqueror. If Israel stood discredited, and Micah was at the end of his ministry, and the sensual cults of Assyria and other pagan lands were pulling hard on youthful society, as carnal cults have always pulled, the corruption of the young Manasseh can be explained. Of Hephzibah, the queen mother, we know nothing. She may have been a bad influence.

So the horrors of Moloch worship, and the carnality of fertility rituals came back along the path which Solomon had first trodden, and filled the land with their decadence. The fact that Manasseh indulged in uninhibited persecution may indicate that there was a loyal opposition which he sought angrily to crush. Micah 7.1–6 may be the echo of this reign of terror. According to the account in Kings, Manasseh was a being of uninhibited evil. The Chronicler mentions a late repentance, as we shall see.

27 : Manasseh Repentant

2 Chronicles 33

The historian of the second book of the Kings passes by the story of the exile and repentance of Manasseh without comment. The Chronicler takes some notice of it. The former writer may have regarded the bad king's reformation as too tardily, too insincerely, made to merit comment. The fact that one historian omitted, and one included, the kindlier facet of Manasseh's reign seems to have sparked off much discussion among the Jews. Hence a crop of legends of deliverance surrounding Manasseh's exile, and also that small classic of penitential devotion, the 'Prayer of Manasseh', prompted by 2 Chron. 33.13, and included in the Old Testament Apocrypha.

Perhaps the facts are that, careful vassal of Assyria though he contrived to be, Manasseh was involved in the revolt of the viceroy of Babylon, Shamash-sham-ukin, against King Ashurbanipal. It was grimly difficult in such dynastic strife to determine which side to back, and a four-year uprising (652–648 B.C.) by Babylon's royal governor (he was the brother of Ashurbanipal) must have presented problems to Manasseh, which could account for a period of detention for an investigation of loyalty in Assyria, or Babylon, which became Ashurbanipal's headquarters.

It is quite within the bounds of possibility that Manasseh,

in the stress and anxiety of such an incarceration, was led to reassess his life, and his repudiation of his father's faith. Such repudiations of evil are known in the dark hours of the soul. It was too late, however, to reverse a trend of evil now almost two generations long. It was too late, also, to save Amon, Manasseh's son, who bore the name of the Egyptian ram-god, and in his two-year reign carried on his father's programme of evil, rather than his brief epilogue of penitence. Repentance can come too late to cover the wickedness of an ill-spent life, and too late to save the next generation. Forgiveness does not blot out all the consequences of sin. The distance, too, is great between a man's being frightened about his sins and humbled over them. 'Repentance,' said Joseph Addison, 'is the relinquishment of any practice from the conviction that it has offended God. Sorrow, fear, and anxiety are properly not parts, but adjuncts, of repentance.'

28 : Young Josiah

2 Kings 22.1–7; 2 Chronicles 34.1–7; Ecclesiastes 12.1–7

Josiah owed his succession to the throne to the people (2 Kings 21.24). Perhaps the land was weary of the evil of the two preceding reigns. The dates and years are worth watching in Josiah's life. He was placed on the throne as a small child, but must have been under devoted care, for, as soon as he reached an age of discretion and decision, eight years after, he showed his true allegiance to God. Perhaps the hand of Jedidah, his mother, may be seen in this open act of testimony. At the age of twenty he turned with vigour to the cleansing of the land. Zephaniah and Jeremiah, speaking at this time, reveal how necessary this purging of Judah was, and how superficial, incidentally, was the tardy reformation of Manasseh, a decade before.

Perhaps it has some significance that the last of Assyria's great imperial monarchs died about this time—it was 632 B.C. —and this freed the young king of Judah from the fear of foreign reprisals if he took firm action against the Assyrian pagan cults which were rife in the land. It was also in the thirteenth year of Josiah's reign—626 B.C.—that Jeremiah commenced his prophetic ministry.

Josiah was to die unnecessarily and tragically in his middle thirties, but he accomplished much for God as a young man and as a youth. His life is worth studying by young men. He is marked by conviction, and strong, swift action on the drive of conviction. Perhaps it was this swift decisiveness which, in the end, took him to a needless battlefield and to death, but at the ages of sixteen and twenty we see the character of the young king shining like a light in Judah's darkness.

'Youth,' wrote Ruskin once, 'is the period of building up in habits and hopes and faith— not an hour but is trembling with destinies; not a moment once passed, of which the appointed work can ever be done again . . .' It was as though young Josiah recognized this fact, had some foreboding of the brevity of his remaining years, and struck doughtily and well for God.

The Bible is a vast encouragement to all ages. It shows boys in action, girls, and aged men. Youth is the opportunity to become somebody. Josiah was to leave his indelible mark on Judah's memory. One can imagine the shaking of more aged and more prudent heads when the boy king announced his intentions—or simply revealed them. But how true are George Macdonald's words: 'When we are out of sympathy with the young, then I think our work in this world is over.'

29 : Josiah and the Law

Deuteronomy 28; 2 Kings 22.14–20

The ancient roll of Deuteronomy had lain hidden in the rubble that had again, since Hezekiah's cleansing, collected in the holy place. Thus it is that man amid the clutter of his worldliness loses the Word of God. Its provisions none the less abide, and, as Scofield's headline has it, 'by the Law is the Knowledge of Sin.'

Josiah was young, earnest, and impressionable. The dire impact of what he read fell upon him with its full weight, and there is no doubt that the closing chapters of Deuteronomy make stern reading. 'The word of God is living and active, sharper than any two-edged sword,' said the writer of the letter to the Hebrews, and he had such incidents as this in mind.

It was a test of the young king's devotion and faith that

he heard with such open and ready ears the solemn warnings and denunciations of the newly discovered Law; it was a test of his insight that he recognized the present condition of his people; and it was a test of his live intelligence that he grasped the truth, which has engaged the minds of great historical philosophers from Deuteronomy to Herodotus, and on to Spengler and Toynbee—that the rise and fall of nations is according to a normal law.

Such a story cannot be read today without the same reaction, indeed, without the same deep misgivings. The Law is lost again, amid the rubbish of an epoch, beneath the din of modern living, amid the noisy and the exhibitionist infidelities of those whose task it is to preach the truth, lost again amid the trash of broken-down standards, derided traditions, and the restlessness of materialism.

Youth found the Law that age had lost. If the book had vanished, discredited, neglected, no longer read, dishonoured in the defilement of the holy place, the principal cause, if one man is to be blamed, is the old man Manasseh, for all his vain seeking, after a misspent half-century, to restore a broken religion. It might well be the prayer of older men and women today, tardily aware of the accelerating rush of a Gadarene society, that youth should recover 'the Law', the discipline of faith, the old moralities, the forgotten Saviour. Josiah stands magnificently, his royal robes rent, before Shaphan the scribe.

30 : Huldah

2 Chronicles 34.20–33

Hilkiah, as the next chapter shows (and it should be read in the franker and clearer language of the RSV), was hardly in fit state to comment on the grim truths discovered in the book. He belonged too intimately to the generation whose craven fears, contemptible compromise, or culpable neglect had allowed the pollution to fill the holy shrine and to cover the saving truth. He was a passive instrument in the hands of whoever ruled, a Vicar of Bray, who could not be expected in a time of sharp crisis to tell the truth.

Huldah was a humble woman, merely the wife of the keeper of the priests' wardrobe, but she was now called upon to join Miriam and Deborah, the two other women in the Old Testament who were called 'prophetesses' in their own right. God always has His faithful, fearless voices, whatever the age of apostasy and concealment of the uncomfortable truth.

Huldah was not unfaithful. She spoke no soft and lulling word. She knew that the Law was absolute, that the provisions could not be revoked. She knew also that God was merciful, and would hear any cry for aid. Indeed, the very chapters of Deuteronomy which had crashed so disturbingly into the peace of the moment contained such promises of grace. She knew, however, that the apostasy of the land at large had gone too deep and too far for any permanent reformation to emerge. The evil which had receded in Isaiah's day was a mounting tide again, and nothing, this time, would stay its flow. The nation was ripe for purging, and in exile it was to find the Word indeed, and be stripped and cleansed of its idolatries.

So Huldah told the truth. She appears from her humble dwelling in the page of Scripture and, her message given, disappears again. The Bible can be its own spokesman, its own unaided interpreter, as Josiah found, but the expositor has his place—or her place, as in this story—and that place is hedged by fidelity. Let preaching be within the circle of the Word. (Some have discounted the worth of Huldah's prophecy [28] by pointing out the fact of Josiah's early death. Huldah promised no length of years, and that premature passing may have spared him the misery he was urgent to escape).

31: Josiah's Reformation

2 Kings 23

Josiah's assault on the bestial cults which had invaded Jerusalem seems to have been almost a single-handed effort. Hilkiah was no help. He had tolerated too much. An 'asherah', or phallic emblem, sign of a disgusting fertility-cult, stood in the Temple. So did the homosexual brothels—not 'by the temple', as in the AV (7). Up and down the land the young royal zealot went, rooting out the signs and symbols of a well-nigh overwhelming paganism. We who live in a similarly sex-ridden age, cannot but admire Josiah's zeal, but at the same time observe the limitations upon his effort. The doom

45

of the ancient oracle, according to Huldah, was only post-
poned, and this can only mean that Josiah cleansed the land
rather by his authority than by the co-operation of a changed
and repentant people. Judah and Jerusalem had been too
radically corrupted by the apostate son of Hezekiah for the
grandson to do anything but stamp out the visible flaunting of
evil. It went, no doubt, underground.

Jeremiah, who lived through this reformation, and saw the
solemn ceremony of the covenant in the cleansed Temple,
was dissatisfied with the results. His eleventh and twelfth
chapters probably express his concern. Jeremiah may, indeed,
as this passage shows, have exercised an itinerant ministry in
the towns of Judah in aid of the new covenant, and he saw
perhaps the sullen resistance of dissidents at close quarters
(Jer. 17.1–11), Jeremiah is permeated with the language and
teaching of Deuteronomy, and he saw with painful clarity
that it was not reformation, imposed from above, which Judah
needed, but regeneration which found beginning in the heart
of each individual man. This was why the Lord called upon
Nicodemus to face rebirth himself when he came doubtless to
ask about the rebirth of the nation. Josiah's movement failed
because he did not carry Judah with him. The people obeyed
because it was expedient to conform.

> Then to side with Truth is noble, when we share her
> wretched crust,
> Ere her cause bring fame and profit, and 'tis prosperous
> to be just.
> Then it is the brave man chooses, and the coward
> stands aside
> Doubting in his abject spirit till his Lord is
> crucified,
> And the multitude make virtue of the faith they
> have denied.

Questions and themes for study and discussion on Studies 25-31

1. Consider Micah 7.8 and how to deal with failure.
2. 'Wherever you see persecution, there is more than a
   probability that truth is on the persecuted side' (Latimer).
   What basis is there for this assertion?
3. 'Late repentance is seldom true, but true repentance is
   never too late' (R. Venning).

4. 'The strength and safety of a community consist in the virtue and intelligence of its youth.'
5. Can there be any genuine movement of revival without a recovered Bible?
6. 'Preach the word . . .' See 2 Tim. **4**.1–5.
7. Jeremiah's acquaintance, especially in his early chapters, with the text of Deuteronomy.
8. God's permissive will in history.

THE LIFE OF CHRIST

The Galilean Ministry (1)

32 : The Healing of the Official's Son

John 4.43–54

There is deep Divine irony in v. 44. Though it is not expressly stated, we can be sure that one of the main reasons for Jesus' rejection in Judea was the belief that He was a Galilean, cf. 7.52. Nazareth rejected Him (Luke 4.16–30) because it thought it knew all about Him; Judea because it did not know enough. The Galileans' enthusiasm (45) probably came in the first place from local pride. It is worth noting how seldom Christian artists really portray Jesus as a Jew.

It is often suggested that the story of the court official's son is merely a variant of that of the centurion's servant (Matt. 8.5–13; Luke 7.1–10) but there is no vestige of evidence for the theory. There is no reason for thinking the official was a Gentile, but the centurion probably knew him and so derived his confidence in Jesus. A useful study is Jesus' hard sayings; with v. 48 we might compare Matt. 15.26; 17.17; Mark 3.33–35; 10.18; Luke 9.57–62. We have to know a person very well before we venture to interpret his words; Jesus understood what people meant, not what they seemed to say; cf. John 2.25.

The official thought that Jesus was one of those inexplicable persons possessed of para-normal powers divorced from any obvious moral purpose, a miracle worker of the type Satan had tempted Jesus to be (Luke 4.9–11). Jesus told him He had come to create faith, not work miracles, which do not necessarily produce true faith. Perhaps he had formerly been like Naaman (2 Kings 5.11); now he threw himself on Jesus' mercy and believed the simple word spoken (49 f.). Something of the greatness of his faith may be judged by the fact that it is about twenty miles as the crow flies from Cana to Capernaum.

It can hardly be chance that the first two signs given us by John are among the least comprehensible of Jesus' miracles. Even where we have no wish to deny the miraculous, we are often glad to grasp at semi-scientific explanations. These two warn us that we gain little by such efforts. John, giving the seventh sign, makes it clear that Jesus was acting as God's representative, that it was the Father acting at His request (11.41 f.). We by our prayers act on others for their good at any distance. Jesus, the perfect Man of prayer, received the perfect answer.

33 : The Call of the King

Mark 1.14–20 (Matt. 4.18–22; Luke 5.1-11)

John had finished his forerunner's work; there remained only for him to seal it by suffering and death. Jesus could now begin His full activity. In one way His message was the same as John's; both said, 'The kingdom of God is at hand' (15, Matt. 3.2), or better, 'The kingdom of God has arrived' (Phillips), for it had come in the person of the King. But Jesus added 'the gospel'. It was not given to John fully to grasp how the Judge could also be the Reconciler. The gospel was essentially Jesus Himself; He displayed by His actions God's good will to men, and for those with eyes to see He showed that He was the King.

A king without subjects is a contradiction in terms, and so in Mark we are early introduced to His full-time disciples. All four had first come to Him through the Baptist, directly or indirectly. Then, however, it was an introduction; now came the kingly call to committal. The natural inference from the story of the Temple tax (Matt. 17.24–27) is that only Jesus and Peter were liable to the tax, a liability that began at twenty. This is supported by consistent Church tradition that Peter was the oldest of the disciples, and he is the only one of them whose wife is mentioned in the Gospels (Mark 1.30).

In the great spiritual changes that have influenced the Church the original insights have, more often than not, come from older men, but they have normally been carried through by younger men. Utter loyalty to Christ does not by itself create the flexibility of mind needed for new concepts. Jesus was also respecting the claims of family life in calling mainly unmarried men to abandon their normal responsibilities. Taken in a wider setting John 2.12 suggests that Jesus arranged for His mother and brothers before beginning His full ministry, cf. John **19**.26 f. Far too many young people today create responsibilities for themselves before they know Christ's purpose for their lives. If Jesus did not marry for our sakes, we can defer marriage a little for His.

Those who admire acting on the spur of the moment should ponder the fact that Peter was able to fall back on his boat and nets when he needed them (John **21**.3). In addition, it should be obvious that James and John had told their parents of their earlier experiences with Jesus. There is no reason for thinking that Zebedee was not in favour of their following Jesus' call, cf. Matt. **20**.20.

34 : The Return to Nazareth

Luke 4.14–30 (Matt. **13**.53–58; Mark **6**.1-6)

Though its outcome was similar, the visit described in Matthew and Mark must be clearly distinguished from the earlier one told us by Luke. Here we find that Jesus revisited Nazareth quite early during His ministry; we may even infer that He had not yet called His disciples, cf. Luke **5**.1–11. The fact that He had recently moved to Capernaum (John **2**.12) may well have created a background of ill will, cf. v. 23. In addition, in a society where social position was largely fixed by land-ownership, the landless carpenter was looked down on. Jesus had not yet become famous, though for Nazareth He was a seven-days' wonder. They offered Him the honour of the reading of the prophetic portion, which followed that of the Law (there was no fixed lectionary at the time). This honour included the right of preaching the sermon, which was done sitting down as a mark of the teacher's authority.

Luke gives us only the vital part of the reading and the central thought of the sermon (21), which must have been of considerable length and conforming to the pattern of Mark **1**.14 f. The reaction was, 'What a wonderful sermon to come from *him*!' (22). Jesus told them that because they were not prepared to accept Him as God's prophet, i.e. spokesman, cf. Exod. **7**.1 f., they could not reap the benefit of having a prophet in their midst. They showed their incomprehension by treating Him as a blasphemer—throwing over the edge of the hill was the first step in stoning. Once out of the town Jesus just 'walked straight through them all' (NEB), as they were suddenly struck by the full impact of His character, cf. John **8**.59; **10**.39; **18**.6.

On His later visit Jesus came with His disciples (Mark **6**.1) and gave some considerable teaching (the force of the Greek in Matt. **13**.54). Fancied familiarity still bred contempt, but now there was no attempt to vent their anger on Him. The result, however, was the same. They excluded themselves from experiencing the power of God in their midst. These two incidents show how completely Jesus had veiled His powers and glory during the long years in Nazareth, while He was waiting for His Father's call. On the other hand, it is most likely that James' description of true religion (**1**. 27) was based on his memories of his older brother's life during that time.

35: The Authority of Jesus

Mark 1.21–42 (Matt. **8**.1–4, 14–17; Luke **4**.31–44)

We are here introduced to the main bone of contention between Jesus and the Pharisees. Orthodox Jewish teachers have always disclaimed any authority beyond that inherent in the Law and the consensus of their fellow teachers. The 'ordination' of a rabbi is no more than the recognition by a number of recognized rabbis that he has sufficient knowledge of Law and tradition to expound them. Examples of Jesus' authority in teaching are found both in a passage like Matt. **5**.17–48 and in His general attitude. This involved the rejection of the scribes and Pharisees as authorities—though not necessarily of their teaching, cf. Matt. **23**.2 f.—and so they rejected Jesus.

His authority in matters spiritual was confirmed by His authority over spirit beings (23–26). There follows His authority in the realm of creation. In the story of Peter's mother-in-law we find a touch that constantly recurs and which for a doctor is far more puzzling than the miracles themselves. Growing stress is laid today on the 'psychosomatic' nature of much illness, and so the possibility of spiritual healing is increasingly accepted. This cannot explain that none of the debilitating effects of a high fever was seen (31); this shows the power of the Creator.

The crowds, without realizing the deeper implications of Jesus' presence, saw that there was the golden opportunity for healing (32 f.). They waited until sunset so as not to profane the Sabbath. Matt. **8**.17 makes clear that Jesus did not heal simply by a word of power. On the cross He identified Himself with human sin to destroy it; in *life* He identified Himself with human sickness to destroy it. We infer from vs. 38 f. that what happened in Capernaum was typical of events elsewhere.

Leprosy, not necessarily identical with the disease so called today, but rarely curable (Lev. **14**.2), was chosen by God as a picture of human sin in the defilement it caused. Jesus not only healed, but by touching the leper demonstrated that He could not be contaminated by his impurity. The leper's presenting himself to the priest would be not merely a proof of his healing, but also that God had sent a Healer. We sometimes stress the guilt of sin to the exclusion of its defilement, which is just as evil; it is particularly stressed in Ezekiel and Hebrews. Jesus has dealt equally with both.

36 : Authority to Forgive

Mark 2.1–17 (Matt. **9**.1–13; Luke **5**.17–32)

From leprosy, the outward picture of sin, Mark passes to sin itself. Some details of the story are difficult to fill in. If the RV mg., RSV, NEB are correct in rendering 'at home' (1), the house cannot have been the larger building postulated by some commentaries but a one-roomed structure, with a flat, earthen roof, supported by matting resting on cross-beams. To dig a hole through did not imperil those underneath, and the damage could be easily repaired. No indication is given of the paralytic's sin, nor why his friends had such a sense of urgency.

'My boy'—'son' is too formal—'your sins are at this moment forgiven,' said Jesus, thereby making it clear that it was their faith (5) that had led to this. Clearly enough the paralytic was, at least for the moment, satisfied by the unexpected words. But the theologians present (the scribes, v. 6) immediately thought, 'Unscriptural! blasphemy!' Jesus did not question their unimpeachable theology, but proclaimed Himself 'Son of man', clearly looking to Dan. **7**.13, where 'one like unto a son of man' is given authority on earth as God's representative. Jesus claimed that this authority covered the forgiveness of sins. Obviously it is equally easy to say,

'Your sins are forgiven' and 'Rise'; equally obviously for those present both would have been equally ineffective. Jesus' ability to cure the paralytic with a word was proof to those willing to believe that the same word of power could cure the sin that lay behind the disease. Clearly, however, the crowd was more impressed by the healing than by the possibility of sins forgiven.

It is not chance that all three Synoptics, with all their willingness to change order, put the call of Levi (Matthew) immediately after the healing of the paralytic. Once one has compromised oneself, as Matthew had, by getting into despised and wrong surroundings, it is often as hard to free oneself as it was for the paralytic to walk. Indubitably Matthew had heard Jesus more than once, and his longing for something better had been easy to read. We must not picture him leaving money and accounts lying about to follow Jesus. He will have been sitting with other collectors near the custom house—the force of the Greek preposition—waiting to go on duty, or having just finished it. The Pharisees were of course correct; 'Bad company corrupts good morals' (1 Cor. **15**.33). But just as a doctor is not restrained by fear of infection, when called to a sick man's side, so the Christian will allow the Spirit to lead him into company he would not normally dare to enter.

37 : Man's Law and God's Activity

Mark 2.18–3.6 (Matt. **9**.14–17; **12**.1–14; Luke **5**.33–6.11)

Fasts among the Jews could be regular statutory ones, private ones due to special grief, and regular private fasts, cf. Luke **18**.12, mainly because of the prevalence of public sin. The last gives the background of v. 18. Rabbinic law forbade fasting among those taking part in a wedding, which could not be held on a statutory fast day. Jesus' answer was the more apposite because the Messianic period was compared to a wedding, cf. Rev. **19**.7–9. Many take 'they will fast in that day' as a command for Christian fasting—something permissible—but the parables of the patch and the wine-skins make this improbable. Christianity is something so new that Old Testament yardsticks are irrelevant for measuring conduct.

The Pharisees objected to the action of Jesus' disciples—

note that Jesus did not do it—because they were technically reaping and threshing (Luke **6**.1) on the Sabbath. In fact, there was here by Rabbinic tradition a clash of duties, for in honour of the Sabbath a man should avoid hunger (Matt. **12**.1). That explains Jesus' reference to David's action and to the priests' service in the Temple on the Sabbath (Matt. **12**.5). Clashes of principle occur more often than we sometimes allow. Jesus then laid down two principles. The Sabbath is God's gift to man, and the Son of man, as God's representative, is the One who shows how the Sabbath is to be used. Since the Pharisees considered that legal interpretations were to be made by the majority in the light of the past, this was a denial of their authority.

The Rabbinic interpretation and development of the Law were normally far more sensible than is generally granted. They laid down that a doctor should not be disturbed on the Sabbath unless life was at risk—a rule many doctors would welcome today. The man (1) was not in pain and had doubtless grown accustomed to his disability. This made him an excellent test case. Jesus turned the point by introducing the antithesis of 'good' and 'harm', or 'save life' and 'kill'. Where we can affirm the former, we are in the realm of Heb. **4**.10. Jesus was entitled to deal with the man, because He knew He could do good and save life.

Hatred creates strange bedfellows. The Pharisees loathed the Herodians even more than the Sadducees, but their greater rejection of Jesus brought them together. The Herodians knew that Jesus' principles meant the rejection of Herodian ideals.

Questions and themes for study and discussion on Studies 32-37

1. What differentiates great faith from weak faith?
2. Jesus called His men *in* their own terms ('fishers of men') but *on* His. What can we learn from this in preaching the gospel to others?
3. Find biblical illustrations of the truth declared in Luke **4**.24.
4. What is spiritual authority?
5. Why did the scribes react so adversely to Jesus during His ministry?
6. Consider the Epistle to the Galatians as amplifying the thought of Mark **2**.21 f.

CHARACTER STUDIES

38 : Prophet Nahum

Nahum 1, 2, 3

Somewhere in Josiah's day, the poet and prophet Nahum finds a place. We may, in fact, envisage something of a revival among the youth of Josiah's own young generation. Nahum, Zephaniah and Jeremiah may have been among the ardent spirits, mere boys and youths, who both caught and fed the flame for renewed uprightness and pure religion in Josiah's early reign. Perhaps there is vast encouragement in the fact for today.

Nahum wrote when the yoke of Assyria was still unbroken (1.13). This would place him before the death of the powerful Ashurbanipal, who died, after a reign of forty-two years, probably 627 B.C. No one could foresee at this time that Assyria was doomed, and that fifteen years later, in August 612 B.C., the city of Nineveh would fall, and that within two or three more years after that fateful date, the bully of the north would lie low—only to be replaced by resurgent Babylon. And that is the theme of Habakkuk's sorrow.

Probably the invaders were already closing in on the great complex of associated villages which Jonah visited, breaking down the irrigation dykes, and terrorizing the land, when Nahum wrote his 'taunt-song', as the Hebrews called such poetry of denunciation. And poetry it is. It is full of flaming language. The very noise of siege, street-fighting and destruction rings through Nahum's vivid poems. Quick, short lines are in harmony with the violence they foretell. The imagery is strikingly colourful.

But we seek the man behind the words. What was the young poet like, who could so cry in exultation over the fall of a mighty city? Consider such language in the light of the Assyrian inscriptions, which boast of genocide, the torture, enslavement and massacre of vast multitudes. No race in antiquity matched the Assyrians for sadistic cruelty. Her wolfish kings were demons of death.

Here was a man who knew the ardour of the group which

55

had discovered the Law afresh. In faith he laid hold of the theme of God's deliverance. Perhaps he marked the growing threat to the wide borders of the gangster kings, and saw, in triumphant confidence, the certainty of imminent divine judgement. The two poems on the fall of the evil city (**2, 3**) are significantly appended to the opening chapter on the greatness of God. They best will understand Nahum today who have lived long, wearing, terror-stricken years under the power of tyranny. It is not wrong to rejoice in the overthrow of hideous evil and foul tyranny.

39 : Young Zephaniah

Zephaniah 1 and 2

If the Hizkiah (as it is literally) of the opening verse is Hezekiah the king, Zephaniah is the great-great-grandson of one of the great reforming monarchs of Judah. A little arithmetic will show that, if Hezekiah died in 695 B.C. and the eldest son of Hezekiah was twelve years of age at that time, Zephaniah can hardly have been much past twenty years of age at the time of Josiah's great religious reforms. Have we then another young poet to set with Nahum, another who like the king, and some other youthful members of the royal circle, laid hold of the words of Deuteronomy, and cried out against the oppressor, Nineveh (**2**.13–15)?

Youth seems to have called strongly to youth in Josiah's day, but not without the heritage of age (Jer. **1**.5). Zephaniah's forbears are given for four generations, and with one exception 'Yahweh' ends their names. These were the days when names were bestowed because of their moral and spiritual significance. Zephaniah's own name means 'Yahweh has hidden', and suggests that his birth may have taken place in Manasseh's Reign of Terror when he filled Jerusalem with blood (2 Kings **21**.16). The young prophet, then, belonged to a true family, whose tradition kept the name of God alive in an age of shocking backsliding.

Jerusalem, the corruption of its city life, the cynical apostasy of its inhabitants, horrified Zephaniah as it had horrified another aristocratic prophet, the great Isaiah. In the opening verses of Zephaniah we see almost as much of Jerusalem as we see in the whole of Isaiah and Jeremiah. His indignation, like the indignation of the young, is ardent, unsparing, uncompromising, frank.

His style also shows the man. He is a city-man, and there is no flash of the country-side in all the imagery of his book. George Adam Smith writes: 'There is no hotter book in all the Old Testament. Neither dew, nor grass, nor tree, nor any blossom lives in it, but it is everywhere fire, smoke and darkness, drifting chaff, ruins, nettles, salt-pits, owls and ravens looking on desolate palaces . . . There is no prospect of a redeemed and fruitful land, and only a group of battered and hardly saved characters. A few meek and righteous are hidden from the fire and creep forth when it is over.'

Perhaps Zephaniah died young. Perhaps indignation and zeal for truth burned his frame away—a youthful Savonarola.

40 : Josiah's End

2 Chronicles 35.20–27; Lamentations 4

'Nothing is more rare in any man than an act of his own,' said Emerson cryptically. He meant that few men act independently on the strength of a conviction. That is what Josiah did, and he drove much evil from the land. But although he does not seem to have carried the bulk of the population with him, he does appear to have gathered a small group of intelligent and devoted men about his person. We have met two. We shall meet another.

Josiah appears to have enjoyed thirteen years of prosperity and peace after his own great reforms. No doubt the land knew beneficent and righteous rule. Then came disaster by an unexpected series of events. With the death of Ashurbanipal in 627 B.C., the decline of Assyria, as we have seen, began. The evil empire passed into weaker hands, and Nineveh, its vital heartland, fell in 612 B.C.

It was soon after this date that Pharaoh Necho the Second, under whom Egypt was moving into one of her periodic cycles of prosperity and expansion, decided to give the final blow to the rival empire of the north. He marched on Assyria, and appears to have used Egypt's new naval power to bypass Palestine. He could not leave unheld the great marching-route of armies, the pass of Megiddo and the Esdraelon Plain, so he landed his army at Dor. A map will show that Josiah could intervene on Assyria's part only at Megiddo. The Pharaoh appealed to him, in God's name (35.21 f.), to stand aside and give him right of way. Josiah stood firm and tragically died.

Why? Assyria could no longer command him. His own friends, Nahum and Zephaniah, had pronounced her doom. Perhaps he misread such promises as Deut. 31.1–8, and rashly expected to prevent the power of Egypt replacing that of Assyria. Whatever happened, he acted impetuously, without God's clear guidance, when he should have done nothing, but allowed God to act.

Disaster befell, and new subjection. Necho occupied Jerusalem and set up a puppet government. Jeremiah pronounced a dirge over the young king he had loved. And the cynics and the pagans, who had never believed Deuteronomy, had grist for their mills of blasphemy. How essential it is to know when to do nothing! Necho's triumph was destined for the briefest life.

Questions and themes for study and discussion on Studies 38–40

1. Nahum's quotations from Exodus (Nah. 1.2, 5) and Isaiah (Nah. 1.15).
2. Indignation against sin. What are its limits?
3. Can you suggest other Bible characters, beside Josiah and Peter, who acted impetuously?

THE LIFE OF CHRIST

The Galilean Ministry (2)

41 : The Choice of the Twelve

Luke 6.12–26 (Matt. **10.**2 6; Mark **3.**13–19)

From passages like Luke **8.**38; **9.**57–62 it is clear that to follow Jesus as a disciple there was needed either His call or permission. There came a time when the number became clumsy (17), too many being taken out of normal life, and they were an embarrassment when hospitality was offered. So Jesus chose an inner circle, their number symbolizing the tribes of Israel, 'to be with Him and to be sent out' (Mark **3.**14)—note the order. So important was it that they should be the right men that Jesus prayed all night. What a comment on our willingness to act on feelings or a 'hunch'. In spite of the prayer the Twelve included Judas. God's answers to prayers may achieve purposes we little guess. The suggestion that Jesus deliberately chose Judas, so that he might betray Him, is spiritually abominable and runs counter to all we find recorded about Judas.

In the choice of the Twelve, though they did not know it, Jesus was making the first preparations for the sequel to His death and resurrection. So the Father gave Him a foretaste of 'the great multitude which no man could number' (Rev. **7.**9) and of the blessing He was to bring (17–19).

The modern preacher is expected to keep records lest he preach the same sermon twice, at least under the same text. Jesus was a teacher and expected to repeat Himself; it mattered little whether He used the same or similar words. It shows lack of appreciation, therefore, to try to 'reconcile' vs. 20–49 with Matt. **5**–**7**, as though they were variant forms of the same address, even though the disciples are being addressed. Jesus was not commending physical need and suffering (20 f.), which could be produced by shiftlessness and sheer inability to cope, nor condemning possessions (24), which could be the fruit of hard work and economy; had it been so, He would hardly have accepted help from the well-to-do (Luke **8.**3). We must understand these beatitudes in the

59

sense of Matt. **5**.3–10—cf. vs. 22 f. with Matt. **5**.11 f. At the same time, without self-assertion and self-confidence instead of trust in God, wealth was improbable; it was unlikely unless there was some sharp practice and extortion as well. Paul expressed Jesus' meaning in Phil. **4**.11 f; we must accept much and little alike from God and use both to His glory.

42 : The Power of Love

Luke 6.27–49

The moment we take this passage, or similar ones in the Sermon on the Mount, as a new law, we find ourselves facing the impossible. Even if we force ourselves to obey, our hearts are disobeying. If, however, we love those mentioned, we shall find ourselves doing as Jesus said, because His love is at work in us. 'Abuse' (28) is too weak; better is 'mistreat' (TEV). The whole section is governed by love (27) interpreted by what we should like done to us (31). Effective nonresistance must spring from strength and be lovingly positive in operation, or it will only harm others.

While human love and generosity always tend to be our response to love and generosity, Divine love springs from the nature of God—theologically we call it grace—and pours itself out irrespective of response (32-36). It is called 'compassionate' (36, NEB); 'merciful' (AV, RSV) is an attribute of the judge, compassion of the Father-Creator. The concept goes back to a Hebrew word derived from 'womb', cf. Psa. **103**.13 f. Our attitude towards others should be derived from our seeing our fellow men with the eyes of a common Father-Creator.

It is true that one who does not criticize is less likely to be criticized (37), but the impersonal passive construction in vs. 37 f, 'be judged, . . . condemned, . . . forgiven, . . . given', in the usage of the time, implied God as the agent. This does not imply the working out of one's own salvation, but that as one shows God's character through Christ's spirit, one has passed beyond judgement (Rom. **8**.1), and there is no obstacle to the riches of God flowing through one.

Criticism being a denial of God's nature—the term 'criticism' is used because Jesus was not referring to lawful and necessary judicial functions—the one who indulges in it is blind and incapable of guiding aright (39). The highest the disciple can rise is to the level of his Teacher, and so we can never do aright what He did not do (41 f). The very fact of our trying is a measure of our falling short!

Sound doctrine and words are always better than false doctrine, but in themselves they do not make a true Christian. They can be based purely on the intellect, but a truly Christlike life can be derived only from being in Christ, from completely accepting Him as Lord.

43 : Jesus' Tribute to John

Matthew 11.2–19 (Luke 7.18–35)

Even though John was 'a prophet . . . and more than a prophet' (9), he was a man of his time, influenced by contemporary ideas about the Messiah, so he was puzzled by Jesus' activity, probably more by what He did not do than by what He did. The question asked by his disciples was oblique (3), partly, perhaps, lest the title Messiah be overheard by Roman and Herodian spies, partly because there was deep reluctance to use it until the work of the Messiah had been accomplished. Jesus' answer was, 'The power of God is being demonstrated by Me, and I have introduced a new scale of values—*the poor* have good news preached to them.' It was left to John to draw his own conclusions (6), but Jesus would never conform to his or others' ideas of what He should do.

Jesus' tribute to John could be paraphrased, 'You did not go to see a time-server and politician'—it is said that politics is the art of the possible—'but one of God's spokesmen, and more than that, the forerunner of the Messiah. That places him higher than those that went before him, but the least of those who enter into the realization of the Messianic rule will stand even higher. His message has inflamed those who imagine that God's rule can be introduced by violence and other human methods. John's message continues and brings to a climax the consistent revelation of the Old Testament. Just as John did not satisfy men's ideas of Elijah's work, so the one whose way he prepared will not satisfy their conceptions of Messiah's work.' There are two forms of spiritual greatness. One is shown by the work to which men and women are called—how great the position of the Christian worker!—and this can be judged in this age. Then there is the greatness of character that will be made known at Christ's judgement seat and not until then.

Man unwilling to do God's will will always find an excuse. Asceticism may be praised until it makes uncomfortable demands. Equally normality, when it rises above man's experience of normality, finds itself rejected. True Christian living will vary between the patterns set by Jesus and John, but in any case will find itself criticized.

44 : The Penalty of Rejection

Matthew 11.20–30 (Luke 10.13–15, 21, 22)

We are in constant danger of forgetting Jesus' words in John 20.29 (cf. 2 Cor. 5.16), and of thinking how wonderful it would be if we could see Him and have fellowship with Him as had His first disciples. In fact, we might well have shared in the general disbelief. This section, the context of which is probably given in the Lukan setting, brings the matter to a head.

1. The better my religion the harder it may be to come to faith. The men of Galilee were better than those of Tyre, Sidon and Sodom, but just because they knew more about God, they found it harder to recognize God's representative.

2. Why then did God not show His signs there, or for that matter, in the great centres of heathen life, in the time of Jesus? Repentance is something very good, but it is insufficient in itself, cf. John 3.5. In Matt. 12.43–45 Jesus gives a picture of how the final result of repentance can be worse than the first. The Bible is full of pictures of repentance that led nowhere. Better the repentance that gets nowhere than no repentance, but repentance based purely on witnessing a miracle is not likely to have the spiritual basis that brings regeneration. It is not chance that in missionary history obvious miracles are normally confined to the early days of a new work; equally, in personal experience they are generally found at the beginnings of a person's contacts with Christ. In neither case does this apply to those signs of God's grace which are manifestations of a change of *character*.

3. Ultimately the knowledge of God is an act of grace (27). Jesus affirms that a true knowledge of God is only through

Him (John **14**. 9). We should always remember that the ultimate nature of the Son, the God-Man, defies human analogies and categories, and has never been adequately expressed in the standard creeds. Hence controversy on the subject is seldom profitable.

4. The rabbis laid great stress on a man's taking the yoke of the Law on himself, i.e. becoming subject to it. Jesus takes the place of the Law (29, cf. Gal. **3**.23–26). With a properly fitted yoke an animal can do far more work far more easily than without it. With His yoke—always made to measure!—we are doing His work. It is a great mistake to interpret 'labour . . . heavy laden' exclusively, or even primarily, of sin.

45 : The Parable of the Sower

Luke 8.4–21 (Matt. **13**.1–23; Mark **4**.1–20)

In New Testament days the sower went in front of the ploughman, who turned in the seed that had been broadcast. The sowing was immediately after the first autumn rains had softened the ground enough for the ploughshare. There was nothing to indicate what lay beneath the surface; not even where the ploughman would leave the right of way across the field. So the parable deals with the soil rather than the sower or the seed. No explanation is given as to why the soil differs. He who proclaims the gospel may not pick and choose, for he cannot know the nature of the soil where the seed is scattered.

Note that no blame is laid on the unproductive soils. There may be moral blameworthiness as a root cause, but it is not stressed. The path (5, 12) remained unreceptive because the ploughshare did not break it up—no question of a metalled road here! The soil above the rock was shallow (6, 13) because the ploughshare had never bitten deep; the limestone of Palestine, so long as it is soil-covered, is soft. The seeds of thorns (7, 14) were there because inadequate attempts at weeding had been made. How do we explain the varying response of the good soil (Matt. **13**.23)? Was it seed, soil, or the environment in the field? It needs little knowledge of life to tell us how many weaknesses are due primarily to heredity and environment, and that if we are not subject to certain weaknesses, it is entirely due to the grace of God. This links directly with our previous portion. However we choose to explain it, behind unbelief and belief there lies God's sovereign activity. Yet we have to balance this with the fact that Jesus Christ died for all (John **3**.16; Rom. **5**.18 f., 2 Cor. **5**.14 f.).

Jesus began His ministry in Jerusalem, but in the midst of pride of place and tradition there was little room for the seed to root. His first message and activity in Galilee was for everyone, but with growing rejection He increasingly turned from general proclamation to the nurturing of the seed in good soil. This, and similar parables, cf. Matt. **13**.1–52; Mark **4**.1–34, mark the turning point. Only to those who had was now to be given. Many exegetes fail to distinguish between Jesus' parabolic stories, which are simple to understand, and the nature parables, which cloak mysteries and unpopular truths.

46 : More Signs

Mark 4.35–5.20 (Matt. **8**.23–34; Luke **8**.22–39)

At the end of a long day of teaching Jesus was tired. So His disciples simply took Him across the lake in the boat from which He had been teaching (**4**.1), cf. NEB, Phillips, TEV (36). Jesus soon fell asleep—the mention of the cushion (38) is a sign of an eye-witness—and was not awakened by a heavy squall that swept over the lake. The frequently met opinion that He was interfering with the handling of the boat by being in the steersman's place is an example of over-refinement in exegesis. Were it meant, it would have been said; the parallels do not suggest it. In any case it would have been out of character. The disciples' attitude is interesting (38); they did not doubt Jesus' power, but His concern. For those in God's service there is no guarantee against drowning, literal or metaphorical, but if one is drowned, it is the working out of God's perfect will (Rom. **8**.28), and hence there are no grounds for fear (40). As with the miracles of healing, the effect was complete (39). Normally the falling of the wind, which could have been entirely natural, would be followed by a period of rough water.

Control over inanimate nature is of value only if it leads

to spiritual results. So the story of the storm-tossed lake is linked with that of the storm-tossed man. The impression created by a legion was, above all, of disciplined power, so the rendering ' Mob ' (TEV) is particularly unfortunate. Just as Israel had succumbed to the might and discipline of Rome so this unfortunate individual had become the slave of the organised forces of evil. Nevertheless, faced with his Creator, his response was stronger than the spirits that had enslaved him. The man was probably a Jew, but since the district was predominantly Gentile, the pigs are not likely to have had Jewish owners. Many suggest that Jesus had no right to destroy the legitimate property of others, but if the drowning of the pigs was necessary for the man's rehabilitation, who will say the price was too high, the more so as God could have restored what was lost? The healed demoniac had to learn to live a normal life (19) before he became a preacher (20), something we are slow to remember. Why the unclean spirits were so anxious to enter the pigs (cf. Luke 8.31) must with our inadequate knowledge remain a matter of conjecture.

47 : The Twelve and the Five Thousand

Luke 9.1–17 (Matt. 14.1–21; Mark 6.7–44; John 6.1–14)

Luke narrates the sending out of the Twelve only briefly, because he gives the bulk of the instructions they received in connection with the sending out of the Seventy-two (10.1, NEB, RSV mg.), whose brief was similar. All three Synoptics mention ' authority ' (1); Jesus gave them as His representatives something of the authority He had received from the Father. Luke alone mentions power as well. In both the Old and New Testaments miracles are recorded which were not from God, cf. Matt. 7.22; 12.27; 24.24; Acts 8.9; 19.13; 2 Thess. 2.9; Rev.13.13 f. Where these powers come from is unimportant, the authority behind them is what matters, and this authority is borne witness to by a Christ-like life. For further treatment of vs. 1–5 see comments on Luke 9.51–10.16 in Study No. 64.

Jesus was ' the second man ' (1 Cor. 15.47), and neither then nor now do men take Him as He is. To identify Jesus with John the Baptist or Elijah (7 f) was an attempt to cut Him down to size and make Him easier to live with. We must always beware of explanations of Christ which have this effect.

Apart from the account of His death and resurrection the story of the feeding of the Five Thousand is the only incident told by all four evangelists. John 6.6 makes it clear that the miracle was premeditated. Its effect (John 6.15, 26) was precisely what He had foreseen in the first temptation (Luke 4.3 f.). Since the long address in the Capernaum synagogue (John 6.25–65) is not hinted at by the Synoptics, this cannot have been the primary purpose of the miracle. This may be hinted at in Mark 6.52 (cf. Mark 8.17–21). It was performed between the entrusting of authority to the Twelve on the one hand and the confession at Caesarea Philippi and the first foretelling of the passion (Matt. 16.13–28) on the other. Before His humiliation of rejection and death they had to realize that Jesus was Lord not only of the storm-tossed sea and the individual but also of man's physical needs, not merely of his spiritual ones. It also brought home some of the implications of His passing on of His authority.

Note that more was left over than had originally been there (17). This rules out any theory of mass hypnosis. The modern idea that the boy's generosity (John 6.9) shamed others into sharing what they had with them bears all the marks of modern sentimentality and accuses the evangelists of deliberate fraud.

Questions and themes for study and discussion on Studies 41-47

1. Jesus chose twelve disciples. Where else in the Bible do we find men being chosen to train for service under somebody else?
2. What is the relationship between doctrine and life?
3. Can we avoid all criticism from the world if we are faithful to God?
4. Why were not the mighty works done in the Galilean cities done also in Tyre and Sidon?
5. What may the preacher of the gospel learn from the parable of the sower?
6. Is there demon-possession today? If so, what are the marks of it?
7. Why do you think all the evangelists record the feeding of the Five Thousand?

CHARACTER STUDIES

48 : Jeremiah's Call

Jeremiah 1.1–10; 2.1–13

Josiah was dead, and Jeremiah, who was to be the greatest and the most tragic of the young men who turned to preaching in the surge of Josiah's day of reformation, lamented him in haunting verse. At this point, we must turn to the life of this great man and seek to know him, for Jeremiah was one of the most Christ-like of the characters of the Old Testament, a man who suffered cruelly for his faithfulness, and whose name undeservedly became a byword for despair.

We must look at his beginnings. Anathoth, called Anata today, is a tiny village just north of Jerusalem, on the first of those rocky shelves by which the central highlands of Palestine fall away into the great cleft of the Jordan. The deep rift makes an awesome landscape backed by the purple rampart of the mountains of Moab, above which each day's sun rises out of the far deserts of Arabia.

Jerusalem tops the ridge, 3,000 feet above the valley floor which lies a bare 20 miles away, and Anathoth was not remote from the restless life of that ancient city. The brilliant son of the village priest of Anathoth, a man named Jeremiah, was conscious of his people's joys and aspirations, which gathered round Yahweh's shrine in the sacred city. He was conscious, too, that a few miles west of his native village lay the main road north from Jerusalem, the old invasion-route and marching-track of armies, the land's link with the northern empires, their pride, their ruthlessness, and their domination.

And grim days were dawning. It was 627 B.C. and the life of the man who was to exercise his sombre ministry in Jerusalem was lived under the shadow of the imperial tyranny of great Babylon. It was a bitter time for a man called upon to preach, especially when the deep conviction which charged his whole message was that Israel's only hope lay, at the moment, in bending before the storm, and abjuring a futile and helpless resistance. Jeremiah's unpopular advice was rejected, and the Babylonian conqueror, Nebuchadnezzar, beat

Jerusalem flat in the prophet's lifetime, burned and looted the Temple, and deported her people.

49 : Jeremiah's Message

Jeremiah 1.11–19; 5.1–31

The message Jeremiah was called upon to give was almost intolerably sad. It was not, however, without ultimate hope. A future lay beyond the desert of suffering, and this is the meaning of the prophet's first vision.

When Jeremiah was called to preach, two symbols, Eastern fashion, filled his mind. One was a symbol of horror, the other of wondrous hope, and the mingling of the two make, in fact, the prophet's message.

In a dialogue with God which makes the poetry of the opening chapter of his book, Jeremiah answers a question: 'What do you see?' And I said: 'I see the branch of an almond tree.' And God said: 'Well have you seen, for I am awake over My Word to perform it.' The English translation cannot produce the Hebrew word-play, and the punning symbolism which makes the point of the passage. The Hebrew for almond tree is *shakedh,* which means 'awake' or 'watchful'. 'I see a branch of the wakeful tree,' says the prophet. 'I am awake,' comes the reply, and the word differs only in a vowel. It is *shokedh*: 'I am awake to fulfil my will.' The almond won its poetic Hebrew name by early blossoming. First of the flowering trees, it sensed the touch of spring, and burst into bloom, to become a sign of hope.

Jeremiah needed the assurance, for the second symbol in his vision was an awful one. 'What are you seeing?' 'A cauldron boiling, and its face is from the north.' This was Jeremiah's image for the fearful menace which overhung the little land. It was the immediate threat. The almond branch was ultimate hope, ultimate, indeed, for Jeremiah's own life was ended before the scalding brew from the tilted pot of Babylon ceased spilling over the land which he loved, and sought, by unpopular advice, to save. The bitter flood consumed his people and sent him into exile. But what his faith had learned, in the twin visions of the almond tree and the seething pot, was that history is not out of control.

But is there not pathos in the picture which forms in the

mind as we seek to reach back through the centuries and understand? Fascinated by the spring's beauty, the boy of Anathoth watches the wonder of life renewed in the almond bloom, and yearns over a dying age.

50 : Jehoahaz

2 Kings 23.31–34; Ezekiel 19.1–14; Jeremiah 22.10–12

The last chapters of the royal records hurry over tragic events and short unhappy reigns as though the narrative had become too painful to write. To comb the brief verses for personalities is to encounter the agony of men, doubt, stress of soul, betrayal, heroism and death.

Shallum, third son of Josiah, succeeded his father by popular acclaim and the enthusiasm of the priesthood, doubtless at this time in the hands of Josiah's reforming party (23.30). Hence the 'anointing', a ceremonial not always observed for the kings of Judah. At this time Shallum must have changed his name to Jehoahaz, which means 'Yahweh takes hold', a testimony to his faith. He was twenty-three years old.

Shallum, or Jehoahaz, as we may now call him, must have been a young man of great promise and charm, for his cruel fate won the dirges of both Jeremiah and Ezekiel. Hence the difficulty in the remark that 'he did evil in the sight of God.' No particular offence is mentioned, and the unfortunate young man had small opportunity to manifest the unexpected flaw in his personality. In some momentous way, he must have shocked and disappointed those who had preferred and promoted him over two older brothers. Ezekiel's lament seems to suggest, in the language of poetry, that Jehoahaz was a young man of vigour, the son of a determined mother. But Josephus, who preserved some old rabbinical traditions, said that the young king proved 'impious and impure in his character.'

The years might have brought improvement or deterioration, but poor Jehoahaz had little time to reveal whatever it was that lay in his heart. Pharaoh was on the march, and after nine centuries, at the end of his drive to the north, Egyptian soldiers saw 'the other river', the far Euphrates. Necho consolidated his Syrian conquest as best he could, and in the course of his activity heard that Jehoahaz had been appointed king in Jerusalem. Perhaps it was the leonine traits in the young man's character, those lauded by Ezekiel, that Pharaoh disliked. At any rate, he took him a prisoner to Egypt. Whether Ezekiel's 'hooks' were literally the hooks in the nose by which prisoners, in the cruel fashion of the day, were led, cannot be said, but Jehoahaz died in Egypt.

No king of Judah before him had died in prison. A veil is drawn over the young man's despair, his pain of body and of mind, the torture of his doubts, his memories of his good father, his agonized prayer . . . Necho's expansionist policies were short-lived. Nebuchadnezzar was a huge shadow on the horizon. Perhaps Jehoahaz died when Babylon threatened Egypt's borders, for Jehoahaz' deposition could have been for anti-Egyptian daring.

51 : Jehoiakim

2 Kings 23.34–24.7; Jeremiah 26.20–23

Eliakim, second son of Josiah, was renamed Jehoiakim by Pharaoh Necho according to a custom of the day. The meaning was the same (' God will establish '). ' Yahweh ', in the name, was merely changed to ' El.' The significance of the change is therefore not clear, but the new name meant as little as the old. The king was twenty-five years of age.

Jehoiakim's sorry story can be pieced together from Jeremiah, who could do nothing with the foolish man. He was looked upon as a puppet of Egypt, and a collector of taxes for the alien, a reputation which he might have countered by a demonstration of care for his impoverished people. Instead, he was a self-indulgent and self-opinionated man, flaunting affluence amid the land's misery. Perhaps Nehushta, daughter of Elnathan, an obedient servant of Egypt, was to blame for his folly.

Pretentious building has often been a sign of royal estate. The Emperor of Babylon, the Nebuchadnezzar of the story, was to rebuild the mighty Euphrates city to express his pride. Solomon had done no less in Jerusalem. But Jehoiakim's Jerusalem, and Jehoiakim's times, were not such that self-glorifying expense was appropriate, or a mark of worthiness. Habakkuk, whom we are soon to meet, expressed the mood of the day in words directed against Nebuchadnezzar, but finding imagery nearer home (Hab. 2.9–11).

Crime was added to folly when Uriah was extradited from Egypt at the hands of Elnathan, and murdered for speaking out.

In Jehoiakim's fourth year Nebuchadnezzar, in the strife of the two empires, Babylon and Egypt, tore Judah out of Egypt's hands, and Jehoiakim acknowledged his dominion. But Nebuchadnezzar, preoccupied with his own establishment in Babylon, was out of range of Judah for three whole years, and, gaining rash confidence, and persuaded by Egypt, Jehoiakim rebelled. It was against the most solemn advice of Jeremiah (Jer. 36.29). It was Judah's perennial fault in those days to be seduced by Egyptian promises.

Hence doom and disaster; Jehoiakim was carried off to death, and the Chronicler makes a strange remark about some sign of evil on his person (2 Chron. 36.8, AV[KJV]). Was it a heathen tattoo-mark? Few rulers of Judah have passed from the pages of history loaded so heavily with scorn, The times called for humility and hearkening to God. Jehoiakim was vain, and deaf.

52 : Foolish Jehoiakim

2 Chronicles 36.1–8; Jeremiah 22.13–19

We have seen the vast problem in foreign relationships which Jehoiakim faced. There was the powerful prince of Babylon, absent but aware of events to the south of him. There was Egypt, beaten back from her ambitions of a decade's renascent militarism and expansion. Which was he to follow? For Judah's helplessness there was Jeremiah's third course.

Between the imperial millstones Judah's hope was only in non-alignment. No moral issues were involved, as they sometimes are in international affairs. Non-alignment in Jeremiah's day was sense, because among the warring nations Judah's contribution to human culture was the vital element in history. The giants were sterile. The little land had something to preserve.

And at such a time, with the control of Palestine see-sawing between the two imperial powers, a young fool on the throne chose to oppress his subjects and parade his wealth.

Light has recently been thrown on the sordid reign and the royal ostentation.

An archaeologist of the Hebrew University at Jerusalem has uncovered a palace of Jehoiakim, which makes him look like a Jewish Nero who fiddled while the fires swept down on Palestine.

Jehoiakim appears to have died on the way to captivity, as we have seen, at the age of thirty-six. He reigned over the menaced land from 609 to 598 B.C. and left a name of contempt behind him. The ruins of his great palace stand in the fields of a kibbutz on the old Israel-Jordan frontier to illustrate the statement. The archaeologists found that, to make room for the king's ostentatious dwelling, a peasant village had been obliterated, after the fashion of the Norman kings' burning of Saxon settlements in England to make the New Forest.

Hence Jeremiah's denunciation in 22.13–19. He refers here to the untimely building projects of the young king.

The excavations support the description. The great outer walls, nine to twelve feet wide, enclose a five-acre compound. Its fine squared stonework is only equalled in Palestine by the masonry of Ahab's palace in Samaria. The windows to which Jeremiah refers were of unusual magnificence. Architectural fragments in the debris suggest that they were enclosed by decorated columns. A most powerful impression of strength and magnificence must have been created. And all this under the black shadow of war.

Jeremiah's moral indignation at the sight was aroused by something more than the forced labour which the arrogant young king must have used. To strut thus, and flaunt wealth and tyranny, was sin in such a twilight.

53 : Jehoiakim's Folly

Jeremiah 36

For a last vivid glance at Jehoiakim we can find our way to a room in the palace which the young king had built. It was winter, possibly the winter of 605 B.C. In such a season ancient war found pause, but policy was made. Jehoiakim was considering the problem of Babylon and Egypt, a dilemma beyond the power of his mind.

For all that, had he been a man of God, able and ready to recognize the leading of God, there was the course which Jeremiah recommended, unheroic in the eyes of some of the royal counsellors, but sane. Sitting safely amid his wealth, Jehoiakim, vain and self-assured, was counting up the cost. Nebuchadnezzar appeared silent and remote. Pressure was applied by Egypt, whose Pharaoh after all had put him on the throne. Policy was veering to the south. Jeremiah was loud in warning, and the young king hated him for it. The story is in the vivid thirty-sixth chapter of Jeremiah's book . . .

Jehudi, the scribe, read out to the king the prophet's menacing words. The king sat in his private room, and it was, as we have said, winter, with a small brazier burning by his chair. It took place, no doubt, in the fine new palace. Not liking the words, the king petulantly seized the roll from the reader, drew his dagger, and slashed it. He dropped it contemptuously in the blazing brazier beside him.

Truth is not destroyed by burning the written or printed words which give it body and voice, or even by persecuting and killing those who hold to it, as Jehoiakim had murdered Uriah, the other faithful counsellor. The chapter ends with sinister words:

> 'Jeremiah took another scroll and gave it to Baruch the scribe . . . who wrote on it at the dictation of Jeremiah all the words of the scroll which Jehoiakim king of Judah had burned in the fire; and many similar words were added to them.'

Jehoiakim, against sane advice, rebelled, challenging the ruthless king of Babylon. It was a simple matter for the royal armies of such an imperial power to overrun the little state, and Jehoiakim went away in chains, leaving his red cedar ceilings and his great windows. Nebuchadnezzar had him killed, and his body was flung outside the wall, 'the burial of an ass' (**22**.19), as the hated prophet had foretold, 'cast out to the heat by day and the frost by night' (**36**.30).

The stone walls of Jehoiakim's ostentatious palace south of Jerusalem are a sad memorial to folly and arrogance.

Questions and themes for study and discussion on Studies 48-53

1. Jeremiah was called to preach submission, or at least non-alignment. Isaiah was called to preach resistance. Why the difference?
2. Can truth be suppressed?
3. Ostentatious living and Christianity.
4. How is advice to be tested?
5. Josiah's sons. Why does a younger generation sometimes abandon its religious tradition? Is it the fault of defective transmission?

THE LIFE OF CHRIST

The Galilean Ministry (3)

54 : Further Miracles

Matthew 15.21–39 (Mark 7.24–8.10)

Herod had been showing an unhealthy interest in Jesus (**14**.1 f.), and the Jerusalem religious authorities had challenged Him (**15**.1 f.), so He moved to areas outside their control (Mark **7**.24, 31). The NEB, Jer. B., and TEV are almost certainly correct in making the woman address Jesus as 'Sir' (22, 25); when she continued with 'Son of David', it is improbable that it meant anything special to her. Even if she was consciously calling Him Messiah, it was something she had picked up from Jews, who were plentiful in the area. Faith is not a blind cry in the night of need, nor is it the use of established formulae; there must be an element of understanding in it, and this she was given by verbal shock-treatment. First Jesus refused to react to a meaningless phrase (23). With v. 24 cf. Matt. **10**.6, Rom. **15**.8; if she had been sincere with her 'Son of David' she should have become a Jewess. Jesus' attitude brought her to her knees as a simple suppliant (25). In saying that it was not right to give the children's food to the house-dogs (26, Jer. B.) Jesus was not creating an either-or. The house-dog can expect to be fed, but cannot choose its food. The woman answered, 'I am asking only for some scraps' (27). Having come to see her position she received her desire. If there seems to be an element of hardness here, see Matt. **3**.9; John **8**.33, 39.

In the area north-east of the Sea of Galilee an unusually large crowd gathered, reminiscent of the early days in Capernaum (Mark **1**.32 f.), because Jesus had not been there before; it may have included many Gentiles. The testimony of the demoniac (Mark **5**.20) may have contributed. In the story of the five thousand we are told that it was out of compassion that He taught them and healed their sick (Matt. **14**.14; Mark **6**.34). Here (32) it is compassion for their hungry condition, especially as centres of supply were distant. So there is no reason to doubt that the miracle was performed primarily because of their physical need. No stress should be laid on the different words used for basket, in **14**.20 (*kopinos*) and in **15**.37 (*spyris*); the difference between them was in material and use rather than size.

55 : Peter's Confession

Matthew 16.13–28 (Mark 8.27–9.1; Luke 9.18–27)

Before they returned to Galilee Jesus challenged the Twelve to make up their minds about Him and then to face what the future was to bring. With the development of His ministry the first stirrings of Messianic hope seem to have died down, for He showed no desire to grasp political power; He was seen as a prophet, maybe Elijah come again as the forerunner of the Messiah (14). To the direct challenge, Peter said, ' You are the Messiah ' (NEB), adding ' the Son of the living God ', which in his mouth meant God's perfect revealer. In the light of John **1**.41 Jesus' reaction (17) may seem surprising. There is, however, a great difference between the confession of momentary enthusiasm, however commendable, and the expression of firmly based and intelligent conviction.

Were it not for the ecclesiastical claims built on it, no special attention would have been paid to vs. 18 f. They are not given in the other Synoptics, and v. 19 is balanced by **18**.18 and John **20**.23, in which the plural is used. More than the Twelve were present on the latter occasion, and the former presupposes far more than the apostles. The obvious interpretation of v. 18 is that the rock is Peter's confession. What we must not do is to find a pun on *petros* (Peter) = stone and *petra* = rock. The use of *petros* for a small stone was unknown in popular Greek. More important is that it was impossible in Aramaic (also Hebrew), which Jesus used. So the NEB translation is correct. Peter was rock so long as he stood on his confession. We need not deny him such priority as he clearly enjoys in Acts; it was limited and not transmittable.

Many moderns think of Jesus' death as a tragic accident caused by evil or undiscerning men. He foretold it, so that accident can certainly be ruled out, but only after the Twelve had realized who He was, lest they thought He had been crushed by the powers of the world. Jesus' obedience unto death demands a similar readiness from His disciples (24–27). Perhaps v. 28 means that relatively few of those present would experience the coming of His Kingdom. Mark 13.32 has been held to rule out a reference to the second coming. An exclusive reference to the transfiguration, resurrection or coming of the Spirit would seem to be excluded by the time-factor, while the destruction of the Temple about forty years later misses the glory implied. It is perhaps best to understand that the whole opening period of the Church's history, culminating in the destruction of Jerusalem, is meant.

56 : Transfiguration and Faith

Mark 9.2–29 (Matt. 17.1–20; Luke 9.28–43)

The transfiguration should be seen as the turning point in Jesus' ministry, even though this had been prepared for by the confession at Caesarea Philippi. Up to this point, in the obscurity of Nazareth and the publicity of ministry, Jesus had perfectly done God's will and had thus reached the goal Adam should have attained. Death had no claim on Him, and presumably He could have gone to the Father at once. The conversation about His departure (Luke 9.31) marked His voluntary going on to the cross. Moses and Elijah (4) appeared as representatives of Old Testament revelation. The transfiguration probably took place on some high peak in Upper Galilee; neither Tabor nor Hermon suit the story. Ponder the discussion about Elijah's return (9–13) for the light it throws on some predictive prophecy.

In the story of the epileptic boy, it is important to identify the people referred to. The faithless generation (19) are primarily the disciples. We should not blame the father for his ' if you can ' (22), for the disciples had failed. ' All things are possible to him who believes ' (23) is not throwing the onus on the father but answering the ' if you can.' All things were possible to Jesus because He believed! The father misunderstood, but his cry with its very human self-contradiction (24) is only a parenthesis ignored by Matthew and Luke. It is in virtue of His own faith that Jesus cast out the spirit.

The disciples' question (28) was, in the light of Matt. 10.1, entirely justified. The contrasting, but not contradictory, answers (29, Matt. **17**.20) show that Jesus' reply was longer than recorded. Matt. **17**.21 (AV) is a later adaptation; the addition 'and fasting' (29) is early but not original. The disciples as good Jews must have prayed before trying to cast out the demon, so it was not lack of prayer but wrong quality that was to blame. Prayer 'in the name of Jesus' involves a claim that we are acting as His representative. This is possible only if we are in living contact with Him through the Spirit and so know His will. Faith is the outcome of living fellowship with God. Behind much apparently confident prayer there is the attitude, 'Well, there's no harm trying.' 'If it be Thy will' is often a more honest expression of lack of faith. The one with true faith will, of course, not start praying contrary to God's nature.

57 : True Greatness

Mark 9.33–50 (Matt. **18**.1–9; Luke **9**.46–50)

The revealing of Jesus' Messiahship, the sense of growing tension and increase in popularity (Matt. **15**.30 f.), and the realization that three of their number had received some special privilege (**9**.2) made discussion on rank in the coming Kingdom a very human reaction (34). Jesus' answer should be read in conjunction with Mark **10**.35–45, where the issue is made even clearer; note the intensifying of 'servant' (35) to 'slave' (**10**.44). What part did the child play (36)? While we should take Matt. **18**.1–4 into consideration, this seems to refer to another case about the same time; indeed the whole section seems to be an outline of longer teaching. The great of the world normally recognize that a reputation for public service helps to maintain their position, i.e. they are serving for what they might get from it. Service given to a child has no reward to expect from the child. Jesus came not to be served but to serve (Mark **10**.45).

The relationship of this to John's words (38) is not obvious until we realize that he was objecting to the fact that 'he was not following US.' This unknown disciple was not detracting from Jesus' glory but from that of the twelve. The Church has always found it hard to come to terms with the Christian worker who ignores its book of rules. If even a cup of water given for Christ's sake has its reward, how much more the casting out of demons, even if carried out unorthodoxly.

The little ones (42) are firstly children, and then the child-like Christian (Matt. **18**.4). Many children have the door to discipleship closed for them by the contradiction between Christian profession and life, and the same has caused many converted persons to suffer from arrested spiritual development. We must take vs. 43–48 seriously, though not literally. The latter would imply that Christ's power is unable to bring the unruly member into subjection. The world clamours for self-expression; the Christian realizes that he is safe only as he limits that self-expression and, in the eyes of the world, maims his personality.

The commandment that salt should be offered with each sacrifice (Lev. **2**.13) was that it should be a reminder of the Covenant (Num. **18**.19). The addition in v. 49 (AV) comes from an early misunderstanding. The fire and salt is the removal of every sign of putrefaction.

58 : Free to do the Father's Will

John 7.1–14

Standing on the mountain top one may well catch glimpses of the road one followed to reach the summit. But many a surprise, many a hidden danger, many a possibility of going astray, awaits one before one reaches the foot of the mountain. The clearer the future and God's will seem to be, the readier we are to make plans, though in fact we have no real knowledge of what awaits us, and so often God reaches His purpose by means we could not have imagined. In this passage we are introduced to Jesus in a position where we might have supposed God's will to be clear. Challenged by His brothers to go to Jerusalem for the feast of Tabernacles, Jesus said He was not going. Behind the statement lay a two-fold meaning. One was that, if He went, it would not be for the motives they had indicated; the time for His arrest and execution, which had to take place in Jerusalem, had not yet come (6). Then, since God had not indicated any other reason for His going, He was staying away. Some days later (10)

God told Him to go, so He went. John's comment 'in private' merely underlines that He was not responding to His brothers' argument.

Such behaviour is so alien to us and to our way of thinking, that in comparatively early manuscripts v. 8 was changed to 'I am not going up yet', cf. AV. A well-meaning scribe thought he had to protect Jesus from the charge of lying. We find James rebuking some of his contemporaries for their light-hearted planning (4.13–16). Some promises about the future and some planning are unavoidable, especially in our more sophisticated and complex society. We should, however, always remember that, except where there is a clear indication of God's will, such planning can mean a limitation of God's right of control. We should particularly beware of commitments which effectively immobilize us until it is too late to respond. We cannot blame the world for creating such situations, though in its attempts to increase the mobility of labour it confesses its error, but the Church should not follow its bad example.

When Jesus arrived in Jerusalem, He found the Divine motivation for the delay. His absence had aroused far more comment than His presence could have. The result was that He had a far larger audience when He began to teach.

59 : The Water of Life

John 7.37–52

It is not certain whether by the last day of the feast (37) the seventh day of Tabernacles is meant, or the following day, which concluded the festival calendar (Lev. 23.36b). The weight of probability favours the former, but our understanding of Jesus' message will not be affected by our decision. Though the custom is not hinted at in the Old Testament, except possibly in Isa. 12.3, one of the chief features of Tabernacles in Jesus' day was the pouring out of water, brought from the pool of Siloam, at the foot of the altar during the morning sacrifice. It was both a thanksgiving that the water had lasted until then and a prayer that the early rains would soon fill their cisterns.

When Jesus spoke, this had been done for the last time that year. So, as with the Samaritan woman, and Jacob's well, He was clearly claiming to be the fulfilment of all that lay behind the water ceremony. As in Matt. **2**.23, no one Scripture passage lies behind v. 38; examples are Prov. **18**.4, Isa. **58**.11; Ezek. **47**.1–12. Perhaps the last fits the picture best, especially if we take it in the light of 1 Cor. **3**.16; **6**.19.

We find in vs. 40–43 perhaps the main reason why God countered Joseph's plan to bring up Jesus in Bethlehem. Not because Jesus was born in Bethlehem was He the Messiah, but because He was the Messiah He was born there, i.e. for the one who, on the basis of His life and teaching, accepted Him as Messiah, there was added as confirmation the fact that His birth had indeed fulfilled prophecy. A Jew may become convinced that all Messianic prophecies were fulfilled in Him, but that does not necessarily make him a Christian.

If the authorities had not ordered His arrest earlier (32), they would doubtless have done so after this claim. When the Temple police returned with empty hands, virtually spellbound by His words, they were rated for preferring a Galilean carpenter to the great men of Jerusalem (48). They discounted popular support and interest by the brutal words, ' As for this rabble, which cares nothing for the Law, a curse is on them ' (49, NEB)—not ignorance but culpable ignorance was meant, but who would want to learn from these proud men? Nicodemus' protest was swept away by the illogical argument that prophets did not come from Galilee (52). In fact, Jonah was a Galilean, but even so, a prophet must be recognised by his message, not his birthplace.

Questions and themes for study and discussion on Studies 54-59

1. Ponder the fact that there must be an element of understanding in faith. Do we treat the teaching element in evangelism seriously enough?

2. Only Peter (or the disciples for whom he spoke) saw that Jesus was the Christ, the Son of God. Do the answers of the crowd show any insight at all?

3. Do you think the words ' listen to Him ' (Mark **9**.7) would have had some special point for Peter in the light of Mark **8**?

4. ' A man often reveals his character when he gets a little power.' Consider this in the light of Mark **9**.35.

5. Is the Saviour's sense of the right time unique or should it characterize His followers, as they follow the guidance of God?

6. John 7.41 f. shows some of the Jews making a false inference from Scripture. Do we do that sometimes?

CHARACTER STUDIES

60 : Jehoiachin

2 Kings 24.6–16; 2 Chronicles 36.8–10; Jeremiah 22.24–30

The king of Babylon set Jehoiakim's eighteen-year-old son on the throne. (The Chronicler's 'eight' for 'eighteen' is a copyist's mistake). He ruled one hundred days, and had little time for evil or for plotting. He was a boy, like the young emperor Nero, dominated by a powerful mother, and it is a fair guess that the queen, Nehushta, was the author of much evil in the land.

There must have been rebellion of some sort. Perhaps Egypt, safe across the intervening desert, and immune from invasion by distance, was plotting behind the scenes again. Egyptian policy has always been to dominate Palestine as a buffer against the north. But Nebuchadnezzar was a decisive man, and was now free from the dynastic preoccupations which had been a temptation earlier to Judah. He knew the ambitions of Egypt, and was now quite determined to destroy any bridgehead that the rival power of the Nile might find in Judah. Hence his decision against Judah.

Jerusalem knew that resistance was useless. The boy-king, along with the queen-mother Nehushta, went out to the enemy camp in pathetic surrender, and the great deportation of the land's strength, talent and wealth followed. Jehoiachin was the Coniah of Jeremiah's words (**22**.24–30) to Zedekiah, and he lay in Babylon, said the prophet, as a sign of judgement on the land. Another puppet ruled over a looted, depopulated, crushed Jerusalem.

The account is too brief to tell us a great deal, and it is difficult to learn much of these hundred days from the two prophets, but tradition suggests that there was something to remember in the hapless youth. One of the gates of Jerusalem, probably that by which he left the city for his thirty-seven-year captivity, was always called Jehoiachin's Gate. Josephus preserves a tradition of kindliness and gentleness. These may have been the qualities which led him to surrender personally to the Babylonian army, to spare Jerusalem. Josephus says that his captivity was annually commemorated. The apocryphal Book of Baruch shows the captive living in Babylon, with a measure of freedom and prosperity, but weeping for lost Jerusalem. We know no more, and much of this is speculation. It is all sad reading, and the stream of divine purpose in Judah seems reduced to a sorry rill—until one remembers Jeremiah and Ezekiel.

61 : Zedekiah

2 Kings 24.18–25.21; Ezekiel 17.11–24

Only a sombre eleven years are left for the monarchy in Judah, and Judah's last king did nothing to adorn them. Mattaniah ('Yahweh's Gift') was the third son of Josiah, and Nebuchadnezzar gave the land one more chance in him. To cement the oath by which he bound him, the Babylonian king changed the young man's name to Zedekiah ('Yahweh's Righteousness').

Zedekiah had little left to rule over, but he had one asset in the prophet Jeremiah. Nebuchadnezzar, no doubt to Jeremiah's sorrow and embarrassment, regarded him as an ally, and a force for peace in Jerusalem. He was—but not in the interests of Babylon's power.

Zedekiah was a weakling. He permitted the reoccupation of the Temple by the abominations which his good father had expelled. Ezekiel, like the exiles generally, seems to have been well informed of affairs back in their lost homeland, and, in his eighth chapter, he describes the heathen horrors being enacted in the holy place. Perhaps many, falling to the bitter disillusionment which we shall see Habakkuk resisting, had lost their faith, and turned for comfort to abominable cults.

If Zedekiah was helpless in the hands of the apostate group who defiled the Temple, he was also unable to resist the princes of the court, who rashly worked against Babylon. Edom, Ammon, Moab and the Phoenicians were plotting against Nebuchadnezzar. Young Hophrah was now Pharaoh of Egypt, and Egypt was busy, after Egypt's fashion, in the background. Such promises bolstered the court rebels. Jeremiah fought bitterly against the folly of their plotting. A false prophet, Hananiah, clothed the conspiracy with lies, and it is the way of all peoples to applaud and hearken to what is pleasant to hear. Hananiah died (Jer. **28**.10–17), and two like-minded 'prophets' in Babylon were burned to death (**29**.21–23), but, persuaded and seduced by others (Ezek. **13**), Zedekiah took up hopeless arms.

In Jeremiah's and Ezekiel's eyes, the burden of Zedekiah's sin was not his inability to see the truth amid the wild babble of conflicting advice and exhortation, nor even a failure to hearken to the true voice of prophecy, but rather the breaking of a solemn oath to the king of Babylon, embedded in his very name (Ezek. **17**.15).

So ended five centuries of Judah's kings. It was 587 B.C. Egypt, as usual, withdrew. The grim story is told, along with that of Jeremiah's shocking ordeal, in chapters **37, 38** and **39** of his prophecy. We may imagine the agony of his mind when he found he could not pray for the doomed land.

62 : Jeremiah's Agony

Jeremiah 37.1–38.4

To the 'hawks' of Jehoiakim's misguided court, Jeremiah's pacifist policy seemed, as was remarked, unheroic and passive. Controversy raged, and Jeremiah suffered all the pain, the traumatic pressure and misunderstanding which brave men suffer when they hold to truth and conviction amid tense and perilous doings. Curiously enough, some potsherds from the guardhouse of Lachish, a fortress thirty-seven miles from Jerusalem, throw light on the scene and on Jeremiah's ordeal. The inscribed shards were the last find of J. L. Starkey, before he was killed by an Arab bandit over forty years ago.

There was an officer named Jaush in charge of Lachish, a bull-dog type who no doubt scorned Jeremiah for 'defeatism', and who seems to have communicated his contempt to a junior commander who held a lonely outpost in the hills. This man was called Hoshaiah.

Hoshaiah saw the force of Jeremiah's timely pacifism, and dared, in the politest terms, to argue with his commanding officer. He had no papyrus. However, there were broken pots enough in any eastern town. He picked up a few pieces on the sidewalk, and wrote to Jaush. Let us quote from Letter Six on the file:

'Who am I, thy slave, a dog, that thou hast sent me a letter of the king to the princes saying "Read, and see that the words of the prophet are not good, liable, indeed, to weaken the hands, to make sink the hands of the men in the city and the country".'

A professor of the Hebrew University of Jerusalem unravelled the text of this ancient court circular. It is strangely relevant, for Jeremiah **38**.4 runs: 'Then the princes said to the king, "Let this man be put to death, for he is weakening the hands of the soldiers . . . and the hands of all the people . . . . For this man is not seeking the welfare of this people, but their harm".'

Hoshaiah begs Jaush to intercede with the princes. 'My lord, wilt thou not write to them saying, "Why should ye do this? . . .".' The letter then breaks off. Hoshaiah probably imagined his senior officer a much more important man than he was.

The earthenware letters came to Lachish, and there was no doubt strong comment from Jaush for his subaltern's insolence in championing the doleful preacher in Jerusalem. But the letters were still in the guard house when Nebuchadnezzar swept down on Palestine.

Nebuchadnezzar beat a breach in the fortress walls by burning all the district's olive trees against the wall. The hole is full of powdered lime and olive-stones. Jaush doubtless swung his sword like a man, and either went down fighting, or went prisoner to Babylon.

His little office fell in ruin.

Great rains seem to have followed, and washed a silt of broken mud-brick through the ruins of the town. Thanks to this, many objects have survived—among them the pottery letters. Two thousand five hundred years go by, and they speak to another age, and throw light on Jeremiah's agony.

63 : Jeremiah's Imprisonment

Psalm 69; Jeremiah 38

Psalm **69** is set down by the rabbis as a psalm of David. Perhaps a careful examination of the language might reveal rather that it was a prayer of Jeremiah, when the enemies of his ministry put him in the disused cistern. It was such a fate as we saw Joseph suffer (Gen. **37**.20–29) but in Jeremiah's case the 'broken cistern' (Jer. **2**.13) was full of deep mud. In such a cruel 'prison' at Gezer a dozen skeletons were found.

There was something furtive about the action of the princes, as though they feared a popular uprising, for Nebuchadnezzar's siege was pressing hard. It seems, too, that Zedekiah was uneasy, and when the brave negro servant, Ebedmelech, hurried to tell him the facts, he immediately authorized a rescue. Zedekiah sent for Jeremiah when the good Ethiopian brought him out, and among the words of comfort, few enough, which Jeremiah sought to give, were words which are almost an echo of Psa. **69**. 'They have let your feet sink in the mud, and have turned away and left you there' (**38**.22). It is a metaphor derived from the shocking experience through which the prophet had just passed, and a strong argument for those who believe that he wrote Psa. **69**. It is a vivid recalling of the awful moment when the sneering faces disappeared from the circle of light above and the stone was replaced—not a tight fit, in order not to check the pouring down of the collected rain-water into the cistern, and to give substance, if Jeremiah did write the psalm, to his reference to flood and overwhelming water, his misery of body and soul.

In the sad narrative of distracted and beleaguered characters, which has been our main reading, we close with two vignettes. Observe that when Ebedmelech went in hot indignation to find the king, he found him at his post where a soldier ought to be—at Benjamin's gate. Zedekiah may have been a fool or a moral weakling. He was no coward in the face of physical danger. Nor was he slow to respond to the brave negro's call for mercy and aid.

And linger a moment over Ebedmelech himself, and his thoughtful collection of used garments from the royal wardrobe to take the cut and abrasion of the ropes as they pulled Jeremiah up—and probably to clothe him as they tossed aside his mire-sodden robes. Said Addison once: 'Half the misery of human life might be extinguished if men would alleviate the general curse they lie under by mutual offices of compassion, benevolence and humanity.'

Questions and themes for study and discussion on Studies 60-63

1. The role of youth and age in the country's affairs.
2. The leadership of youth in matters of religion.
3. Kindness. What is it? How does it differ from mercy?
4. Is taking sides always good?

THE LIFE OF CHRIST

From Galilee to Jerusalem

64 : Reactions to Jesus and His Message

Luke 9.51–10.16

The section **9**.51—**18**.14 is for the most part peculiar to Luke, and he has made no effort to fit it into Mark's framework. Indeed, to assume strict chronological order can lead to an exegetical nightmare. Much in these chapters cannot have taken place east of Jordan.

We may not assume that the Samaritan villagers knew of the events of John **4**.1–42. Their objection was to Jesus' going to worship in Jerusalem instead of at Mt. Gerizim (John **4**.20). Blindness and bigotry can be very annoying—is there any church where they are not found?—but that does not justify our calling down God's judgement on them.

The three men in vs. 57–62 are not types but individuals to whom Jesus speaks 'existentially', cf. **18**.18–23. Was the first (57 f.) afraid of hardship, or was he thinking like Peter (Matt. **19**.27)? Of the second (59 f.) we can be certain that though his father may have been on his death-bed, he was not dead. He was probably mainly concerned that the estate was fairly divided before he followed Jesus. If his father had been dead, the funeral would have been over in a matter of hours and Jesus would never have refused this act of filial piety. We cannot tell the background of the third (61 f.). His parents may have been miles away, or Jesus may have known that he would be unable to resist their entreaties.

With **10**.1–12, cf. **9**.1–6; Matt. **10**.1–15; Mark **6**.7–11; minor differences, e.g. no sandals (4), wearing sandals (Mark **6**.9) are easy to explain—it was a reserve pair that was being forbidden. Seventy-two (1, RSV mg., NEB) is almost certainly correct, i.e. six for each tribe. Though they were not missionaries, as we understand the term, but heralds and forerunners of the expected King, many missionary tragedies would have been avoided, if the principle of pairs, observed also by the Jerusalem church and Paul, had been followed.

The Jews claimed to be subjects of the King of heaven, the heathen to whom Paul went did not, hence Paul could not expect from them what Jesus' messengers had a right to expect in Jewish towns and villages. Similarly, the same drastic action (10 f.) would seldom be justified in a heathen environment, cf. Acts **18**.6.

65 : Rejection and Acceptance

Luke 13.22–35; 17.11–19

The question asked in v. 23 has been a common one at all periods of the Church's history; normally men have not hesitated to answer it according to their preconceptions. Jesus' refusal to answer—Matt. **7**.13 f. is a reference to His own time and situation—should check us. Does v. 29 really suggest only few? What is important is our personal reaction to it. Have I entered by the narrow door?

It is not easy to interpret vs. 31 f. On the whole, the fact that the Pharisees claimed to know Herod's plans and that they were told to carry a message to him suggests that they baulked at murder but would have been glad to see Jesus out of their area. In v. 32 we have a Hebraic idiom for a short time. Clearly, we cannot deduce from v. 33 that all prophets meeting a violent end died in Jerusalem, cf. 1 Kings **18**.4 and John the Baptist. Jesus meant that behind their death lay rejection by the spiritual leaders, who in His day were centred in Jerusalem. For the lament over Jerusalem see Matt. **23**.37–39, which probably gives the original setting, not reproduced by Luke. The same applies to v. 35, which looks to the second coming and not Palm Sunday (Luke **19**.38).

The rabbis interpreted Lev. **13**.46 to refer only to walled cities. In unwalled towns and villages the leper could live so long as no uninfected person shared his house. The boundary between Samaria and Galilee (**17**.11) was never clearly de-lineated, so there were mixed communities in which Jews and Samaritans doubtless kept well apart. A common fate had drawn the lepers together—the Samaritans kept the law of Moses, if anything, more strictly than the Jews. All ten showed faith; all ten were healed. Why did only one come back to say 'Thank you'? The experience of many a travelling preacher might suggest that there is nothing unusual in the proportion. Do you always thank the one through whom the power of God has been mediated to you? Note that the lack of gratitude did not mean the revocation of the healing. Yet lack of gratitude can involve lack of praise to God.

66 : Self-Forgetfulness and Self-Interest

John 11.54–12.11

Ephraim (54, 2 Sam. **13**.23) was an out-of-the-way place some fifteen miles north-east of Jerusalem. It served as a retreat for those avoiding authority, for, if followed, they could melt away into the wilderness. Note that Jesus used normal means to avoid His enemies, who had determined on His death (49 f.). Much in Holy Week becomes easier to understand when we grasp that the common people knew what the authorities intended (56). Those who lived at a distance from Jerusalem normally lived in a state of impurity until just before the great festivals. Some purification, cf. Num. **19**, could take a week, hence the early arrival.

These notes are perforce too brief to deal with the apparent chronological differences between the Synoptics and John with regard to Holy Week. It must suffice to say that if the triumphal entry into Jerusalem (**12**.12) took place on a Sunday, the arrival in Bethany must have been before sundown on the Friday and John has simply ignored the Sabbath, as would be quite natural for a Jew to do when recounting day to day events. In this case the meal would have been after the service, whether in the Temple or synagogue, that ushered in the Sabbath. At such a meal the women would eat after the men (2).

Many efforts have been made to identify Mary with the anonymous woman of Mark **14**.3, and even with Mary Magdalene (Luke **8**.2), in turn linked with the woman of Luke **7**.37. These efforts display more virtuosity than probability. It is far more likely that Mary's action, as spontaneous as the harlot's, whom she had probably never heard of, was imitated a few days later by some neighbour who felt deeply grateful to Jesus.

In fiction we should have been prepared for Judas' outburst and betrayal by indications of his state of mind. John was obviously shocked. Thinking back he will have seen pointers to what happened, but he spares us useless hindsight. How it was discovered that Judas was a thief we are not told. Probably his attitude and betrayal confirmed earlier vague suspicions. When he realized that his ambitions were not to be fulfilled through Jesus, he probably decided to save what he could from the wreck. 300 denarii (5) were nearly a year's wages, cf. Matt. **20**.2. In **11**.50 it was one man to die for the sake of the people; now two were threatened (10 f.).

Questions and themes for study and discussion on Studies 64-66

1. Do people react to Jesus today in much the same way as they did in the days of His flesh? What are the general characteristics?
2. With the help of a concordance trace the word 'Jerusalem' through the Gospel of Luke. It is a word of destiny.
3. Consider the distinguishing marks of fact and fiction, and the presence of the former in the Gospel narratives.

CHARACTER STUDIES

67 : Habakkuk's Doubts

Habakkuk 1.1–2.3; Romans 8.28–39

Before we take a last look at the anguished Jeremiah, and pass on to find other characters of the Old Testament in Babylon, we must meet a troubled man named Habakkuk who wrote and spoke in Judah at the time, it seems, when Babylon was descending on the land. We must try to find the person of the prophet behind the brief pages of his book, a less difficult task than it sometimes is, as we peer behind the words of the later books of the Old Testament.

We cannot be certain of his dates, and the time when he put his agonizing doubts and his triumphant return to faith into Scripture. Some, indeed, have suggested that it was the Assyrian, and not the Babylonian, who was threatening the land, and filling Habakkuk with despair. We can only guess, and hazard a reconstruction of his life, and the framework of experience in which he wrote. We can feel the stir of pity and of understanding for the man who left the little book of meditation and devotion, which goes under his name.

Perhaps Habakkuk was born about 630 B.C., saw the days of Josiah's restoration of worship, and took to heart, along with zealous young men whose names have crossed our pages, the promises of the newly discovered Deuteronomy. They saw hated Nineveh fall, and felt that they lived in such a dawn as Wordsworth described, when it was 'bliss to be alive, but to be young was very heaven'. Habakkuk's dawn, like Wordsworth's own, faded . . .

Habakkuk, if the dates are correct, lived to see Josiah fall under the Egyptian arrow, to see Pharaoh march into Jerusalem and, in the end, see Nebuchadnezzar, the new aggressor, lay hold on the land after defeating Egypt at Carchemish in 605 B.C. Nations were falling before the young imperialist of Babylon. Cities were left desolate as he swept whole populations away to provide labour for his vast building schemes. Jerusalem surrendered her last spark of life in 597 B.C. A year later Solomon's Temple was destroyed.

Where Habakkuk fits in we do not know, but somewhere in this dark chapter of disaster he faced despair. Where, where, was God, the God of Deuteronomy, the God who saved? True, Huldah had spoken, but Huldah was forgotten. Was the king of Babylon mightier than God? Was God helpless in the midst of triumphant paganism? Habakkuk knew the old agony of the good—the biting, searing doubt about the reality of God's promises. Why, O God, why?

68 : Habakkuk's Faith

Habakkuk 2.4–3.19

Habakkuk, in agony over human pain (1.13–15), had seemed to get no light on the problem which obsessed him. He goes to his place of prayer (2.1) and pleads with God. Words come to him which he is constrained to write down. A phrase is put into history (4), which was picked up by Paul (Rom. 1.17), and again by Luther. The vital word is not quite the same as 'faith'. It is the Hebrew *'emunah'*, the word with which 'amen' is connected, and means faithfulness, steadiness, firmness, all of which qualities, of course, are based upon what is understood in the New Testament by 'faith'. The word is used of Moses' hands, 'steady' in the potent act of prayer (Exod. 17.12). It occurs in Prov. 12.22 and Isa. 11.5. Significantly, the Septuagint renders *'emunah'* by the word *'pistis'*, the common New Testament word for faith.

But we seek the man Habakkuk in his message. It was a great soul which, in the hour of his people's twilight and terror, grasped the thought that it is a quality within the heart, a principle of endurance, based on trust in God, which keeps a nation alive, and keeps men and women human when catastrophe falls on a land and on a person. How far was Habakkuk's message known? Did David know his words, and Nehemiah? Read 1 John 2.16 f., as Phillips renders it, for John puts into a verse what Habakkuk grasped as Babylon fell fiercely on Palestine: 'The whole world-system, based as it is on men's primitive desires, their greedy ambitions and the glamour of all they think splendid . . . will one day disappear. But the man who is following God's will is part of the permanent and cannot die.'

On the strength of the revelation, Habakkuk was able to tell what the fate would be of the arrogant and victorious pagan. Five 'woes' will befall, and the moral law will prevail. It is like a preview of the Book of the Revelation. The mills of God grind slowly . . . The harvest, which man has sown, inevitably ripens. Evil battles with the laws of Creation. Habakkuk was the sort of man who is needed today. Such triumphantly certain proclamation is the message for our times. Christians should get to their watch-towers and wait until they know what God will say.

69 : Jeremiah's Choice

2 Kings 25.22–26; Jeremiah 40.1–41.3

Surely no one suffered so hard a lot as Jeremiah. With the departure of the caravan of the exiles, the best and choicest of the land, for Babylon, the prophet faced a choice. He stood high in the estimation of the Chaldeans, and might have lived in comfort in the land of exile. He had been called a traitor, and a destroyer of the morale of his people, and now was faced with a choice and an opportunity to restore his reputation.

Without hesitation he elected to remain with the broken remnant of his people in a depopulated defenceless land, amid poverty, hunger and anxiety. No one, surely, could misunderstand him now! And yet he had abundant motive to justify a retreat to Babylon. Ezekiel was there, ministering to the exiles, and they were the men and women on whom the future of the land depended. Was not this a more demanding call?

Jeremiah made his noble choice, and it was on his recommendation that the upright Gedaliah was made governor of the land and guardian of the daughters of the deposed king. It was probably Babylon's intention to allow him, when the girls grew up, to marry one of them, and continue the line of David. Gedaliah had a difficult rule. He set up his headquarters at Mizpah, north of Jerusalem, a sombre indication of the desolation and ruin in which the capital lay.

The historian of the Kings can hardly bring himself to write of the shocking events which followed. Jeremiah, in a flat, despairing narrative, tells a fuller story. Refugee Jews were pouring back into the land, itself a testimony to the high reputation of Gedaliah. There was a prospect of restoration in the land, a situation, indeed, which the king of Babylon may have overlooked. Whether the prospect of a stronger Israel was a motive for interference from across the Jordan, it is impossible to say, but the villain Ishmael, of sinister name, was sent by Ammon's king to assassinate Gedaliah.

The open-hearted governor was warned, but gallantly refused to credit the warning. He died at the murderer's hands. The bright page of reconstruction in Judah was finished. The dark last chapter of her history resumed its theme. Perhaps Jer. **15**.10–21 reflects the prophet's cry of agony over this period. We cannot say, but the darkness was unrelieved. It was to press yet harder on his hopes and aspirations.

70 : Jeremiah's Exile

Jeremiah 41.4–43.7

Ishmael's iniquity continued at Mizpah. He brutally murdered a small band of refugees who had confidently come to the little town expecting to find the good Gedaliah and, with him, some hope and comfort. And when retribution at last came with Johanan, the scoundrel made good his escape to his master, the Ammonite king, architect of the plot.

Johanan was in a dilemma. He feared the ruler of Babylon, and with his small band decided that flight was the only resort. They moved south from Mizpah, through the ghastly ruins of Jerusalem to the caravan-centre at Bethlehem, a few miles further south, where the name of Chimham, son of Barzillai, David's benefactor, still was heard, and where the Gileadites' tradition of hospitality to exiles still held. So Geruth Chimham became an assembly-point (**41**.17).

Here it was proposed that retreat should be made to Egypt, there to find, at least, some rest from toil, blood and anguish. Egypt had till recently dominated the land, and some hope may have been held that the southern empire might welcome refugees from its hated northern rival. The fugitives were desperate.

Jeremiah now faced another ordeal. He knew that all Judah's hope lay in rebuilding the land, and that every fugitive from Judea was a fugitive from God's task and the nation's destiny. The demoralized Jews professed their willingness to follow God's will. As too often happens to the loyalties of men, there was a hidden condition—God's will was to be followed if it chimed with their desires.

Jeremiah agonized over the problem, and finally found himself convinced that the retreat, even a temporary retreat to Egypt, was wrong. The fugitives turned on him with unworthy charges and recriminations, and Jeremiah's long tragedy of suffering and misunderstanding passed into yet another act. It was hard for such a man to be called a hireling prophet, Baruch's mouthpiece.

Even worse, Johanan gathered up the exiles and refugees who had crept back to the land, following the deportation to Babylon, and a second 'going down into Egypt' was led by him. Jeremiah was forced to accompany them. Could any man have had greater stress of mind thrust upon him? Here we leave him—one of the most tragic figures of history—a veritable foreshadowing of Christ.

71 : Prophet's Call

Ezekiel 1 and 2

Ezekiel's book, like that of his contemporary and elder prophet Jeremiah, begins with a vision set in the language of vivid poetry. In the account he gives of it we see his gift of poetry and catch the ardour of his faith.

'By the rivers of Babylon,' as Psa. **137** reveals, lesser men 'sat down and wept', remembering their far homeland. Ezekiel, by the great irrigation canal of Chebar, saw a vision of God.

The thought of the East is pictorial. Our methods of thought are more at home with the abstract. As a language, Hebrew uses concrete terms in a manner quite unknown in European speech. 'Wall' means 'defence', 'rock' means 'strength', and 'horn' means 'power'. It was therefore easy to render truth pictorially. Hence the language of apocalyptic vision. We cannot enter into a detailed interpretation of the vision of Ezekiel, but it all adds up to a warning that out of the north is coming a destructive invasion—the whirlwind and the blaze of fire. The imagery was found in some mighty desert storm, with billowing sand intershot with lightning. Thus, Ezekiel envisaged, had disaster come out of the north on Palestine.

The rabbis listed man, eagle, ox, and lion as the lords of their respective divisions of creation. 'And yet,' their saying went, 'they are stationed below the chariot of the Holy One.' This is the key. Thus, to those who understood, Ezekiel showed that Babylon's hurricane of evil was permitted by God. If the storm was His chariot, He also controlled it. And so Ezekiel, like Jeremiah, was assured at the beginning of a grim ministry that God was not dethroned, though 'dark is His path on the wings of the storm'.

Human words almost break under the task of showing forth the majesty, the power, the glory of God. It is the vivid and awesome imagery of speed, mobility, purity, mighty utterance and consuming judgement. What were the tawdry idols of Babylon beside this regal Being who filled the sky? From the midst of the flashing symbols of His power came a voice, and it bade Ezekiel stand upright and fearlessly receive a message. The prophet felt strangely empowered to obey. Almighty God needed a man to bear His word, and to speak in His Name to a people. Even in this strange context, the requirements were the same as they ever are—obedience and understanding. Ezekiel was warned against sharing the sin of those to whom he ministered; he was commanded to make the Word of the Lord part of his very being. These demands still stand.

72 : Prophet's Lesson

Ezekiel 3

Ezekiel was promised no triumphant career. He was to preach to an embittered people, and not to flinch before their cynicism and spite. Like Jeremiah, he was called to a forbidding task; and both prophets trod the path the Lord Jesus was to tread. Under the Spirit's strong urging, Ezekiel set out for Telabib. The captivity involved no strict confinement.

Babylon's policy was to enfeeble conquered lands and populate the Euphrates river-plain with the best elements of subject peoples; no doubt the deported Jews lived in many communities with some freedom of movement. One such centre Ezekiel sought for the beginning of his ministry. He went in 'bitterness in the heat of his spirit', but that was not the mood in which to preach God's Word, however stern the message. He sat among them 'overwhelmed' (Moffatt) for seven days. He sat, indeed, 'where they sat' (15), and no man can preach effectively unless he comprehends the pain and the problems of those to whom he speaks. Hence the restraint under which the angry, passionate prophet fell. After seven days of deepening understanding, the preacher was at last in a condition to preach. He was at last effective.

The prophet was set as a watchman and a voice of warning, and the moral responsibility which this task involved was set forth in detail. In spite of it, and with some suddenness, the scene changes at v. 22, and the prophet's ministry is withdrawn at some threat of violence. There may be some lapses of time between vs. 21 and 22; Scripture does frequently make such rapid transitions. It is none the less true enough to experience. The word of warning is disregarded and scorned, and the warning voice is stilled. The Lord had no word to say to Herod, who had long since ceased to hear the voice of conscience; He was silent before Pilate, who had sold his conscience to the priests. So with Ezekiel. The brevity of the narrative conceals labour and rejection, and the consequent withdrawal of the warning voice. It is dangerous not to listen when the Spirit of God speaks to the heart. He speaks only for good and blessing, but presses conviction on no self-willed and obdurate rebel.

73 : Prophet's Hope

Ezekiel 36.22–37.14; John 3.1–8

Ezekiel's great task as he ministered to the exiles was to convince them that their murdered nation could come to rebirth. He had a promise to preach about. It is put vividly in 36.26, 27.

With these words of renewal and rebirth in mind, Ezekiel dreamed a strange and significant dream. He found himself in a valley, or, to be exact, a valley-plain (**37**.1, RSV mg.). Some modern translations, with what appears a perverse zeal to be different, say 'plain'. The word is *'beqaa'*. The Beqaa with the capital B runs up between the two Lebanon Ranges. Baalbek stands at its northern end. Such 'beqaas' are a feature of the land. They are invasion routes, and places of battles.

Ezekiel stood, perhaps, in such a place. The Babylonian armour and their cavalry had overrun some rearguard, and the bones of the fallen lay white and arid among the scrub and wild weed. Here was a picture of Israel, dry, dead, past hope.

The word came: 'Man, can these bones live?' 'Lord God,' replied Ezekiel, 'You alone know'. 'Tell them,' came the Voice, 'that they will indeed live.' Ezekiel did as he was bidden. There was a grisly stirring in the heaps of dead. Skeletons articulated. Flesh and sinews appeared, as the film of time ran backward . . . But they were still dead. Ezekiel is then commanded to call in God's name on the wind. And it must be remembered, if this strange word picture is to be understood, that in Hebrew and in Greek, the tongues of the two Testaments, the same word means 'breath', 'wind' and 'spirit'.

The wind often plays a metaphorical role. The wind in the Sinai gorge spoke to Elijah of the godless surge of life. Job was conscious of the desert winds. It was an east wind that Jeremiah likened to the scattering of Israel. It was by the same wind, rushing out of the burning Arabian desert, as the nor'wester presses down on Capetown out of the Kalahari, that Ezekiel saw the ships of Tyre shattered, and the psalmist the merchantmen of Tarshish. Other winds bring life, and Ezekiel, standing in the Beqaa of Death, must have had in mind the renewing breezes, that, in the north, bring life to the afternoon, or the winds that come out of the west, as they came for Elijah, rain-laden.

Dreams are built of the stuff of life's experience, and in this weird vision to which the Lord obliquely referred in His famous talk with Nicodemus, we catch sight of Ezekiel, his desperate hope, his passionate faith in God's power to transform personalities, history, disaster, and his understanding of what the New Testament was to call 'being born again'.

Questions and themes for study and discussion on Studies 67-73

1. Why do good people suffer?
2. 'Doubt is an experience, but cannot be a way, of life.'
3. Should Jeremiah have gone to Babylon?
4. Is retreat ever justified?
5. Youth and ambition. Can compromise be avoided?
6. 'Sec et' discipleship.
7. Personal experience and preaching.

THE LIFE OF CHRIST

Holy Week

74 : The Triumphal Entry

Matthew 21.1–11; John 12.12–19 (Mark **11**.1–11; Luke **19**.28–44)

We speak of Palm Sunday, but the only mention of palms is in John **12**.13, cf. Matt. **21**.8; Mark **11**.8. Palms do not grow readily round Jerusalem, and their thorns make them unsuited for a spontaneous demonstration. They had either been prepared in advance, or more probably were branches stored from the previous feast of Tabernacles (Lev. **23**.40). This was regarded as a Messianic feast (Zech. **14**.16), and Psa. **118**, as a Messianic psalm, was used during it. Hence the quotation of vs. 25 f. by the people. Hosanna is a popular corruption of *hoshia-na,* 'Save . . . we beseech Thee' (Psa. **118**.25). The most explicit form of the people's shout is in Mark **11**.9 f. Though a portion of the demonstration came from Jerusalem (John **12**.12), many there had no idea of what was happening (Matt. **21**.10 f.), and others joined in only later (John **12**.17 f.), when they knew that it was Jesus who was coming.

This all means that the Galilean pilgrims, both an earlier contingent already in Jerusalem and the main body with Jesus, had made a plot to place Jesus in such a compromising position with the Romans that He would be forced to declare Himself as Messiah. If He was to enter Jerusalem as planned, the only means of circumventing the plot was to seem to go with it, but to empty it of political seriousness by riding on an unbroken, frisky, donkey's colt—its mother was brought along (Matt. **21**.2) to keep it a little steadier. The way the donkey was fetched—its owner was doubtless one of Jesus' adherents —shows that Jesus knew that the pilgrims would have provided a more 'suitable' mount, had they known His plans. Though Jesus was fulfilling Zech. **9**.9, John **12**.16 makes it clear that neither the disciples nor the crowd realized this at the time.

If the question is asked why the Galileans did not call Jesus the Messiah clearly and openly, cf. Matt. **21**.11, the answer is probably that Jewish tradition considered this blasphemy until a person had shown his right to the title—the Romans doubtless understood the meaning of the terms used. If they did not react, it will be because Pilate had ample information about Jesus and as a result considered Him harmless. This comes out clearly in the subsequent trial.

75 : Empty Profession

Matthew 21.12–22 (Mark 11.11–25)

For the details of the cleansing of the Temple see the treatment of John **2**.13–16 in Study No. 21. Here no mention is made of a whip (John **2**.15). The prestige Jesus had acquired probably made His voice alone sufficient.

The order in Matthew and Mark is different. In the former the cleansing follows immediately after the Triumphal Entry, with the cursing of the fig tree on the next day; Mark puts both on the following day (Mark **11**.12). Since Matthew repeatedly ignores chronological order to stress spiritual connections, he has probably done so here also to show the King of Israel as Lord of the Temple. The story of the children (15 f.) is more likely to have happened before the priests were infuriated by the loss of their market. By His quotation of Psa. **8**.2 Jesus, by implication, accepted the Messianic dignity.

The mention of Jesus' hunger (18) shows that we have more than an acted parable. He was looking for the possibility of a few figs having been missed in the autumn gathering, which remained available to the passer-by. In the normal activities of life Jesus went by the same knowledge we all have. Not only were there no figs left, for which the tree was not necessarily to blame, but there was no trace of fruit to come; if there was to be any, it had to appear before the leaves. What followed had obviously a parabolic purpose. Since there is no evidence that the fig tree is used in the Bible as a picture of Israel, in spite of frequent affirmations to the contrary, the curse was a judgement purely on His own generation, which, in spite of its failure and the call to repentance, showed no sign of bearing worthy fruit. It is also a parable for every generation, Jewish or Gentile, where the same condition exists. Some conclusions about the poverty of His friends in Bethany may be drawn from the fact that Jesus was hungry so early in the morning.

Modern man is troubled as to why Jesus should have acted as He did; the Twelve were perplexed as to how His curse worked. Neither we nor they really grasped the lesson. This probably explains the apparently strange sequel in Mark 11.24 f. Forgiveness is one of the main fruits God expects to find as a result of our repentance.

76 : The Problem of Authority

Matthew 21.23–46 (Mark 11.27–12.12; Luke 20.1–19)

We have dealt earlier with the question of authority under Mark 1.21–42 and 2.1–17 (Studies 35 and 36); it lay behind the repeated requests for signs (John 2.18; 6.30; Matt. 12.38). Moses had authenticated his mission by signs (Exod. 4.1–9, 29–31), so it was axiomatic to the religious leaders, as to Orthodox Jews today, that anyone coming, except as an expositor of Moses, would have to authenticate himself similarly. The weakness of signs is (i) that they may come from Satan (Matt. 24.24; Rev. 13.13–15; 2 Thess. 2.9); (ii) normally grounds can be found for rejecting them. So Jesus challenged their willingness to accept through a case where no one suggested the activity of Satan—in spite of Matt. 11.18—viz. John the Baptist. The importance of their response lay in their motivation. Had they sincerely been unable to come to an opinion, it would have shown spiritual obtuseness; their complete indifference indicated their unfitness to ask or judge.

In the parable of the two sons (28–32) the NEB and Phillips reverse the order of the sons, probably correctly, thus putting the one representing the chief priests and elders first. Some manuscripts give the answer 'The second' (31)—using the RSV order. As Schniewind says, this is so absurd and cynical that it is probably correct. We can picture a man like Caiaphas giving such an answer as a refusal to be heckled by a Galilean artisan. John's God-given ability to turn notorious sinners was sign enough. The same type of sign is valid also today, but just as the last word did not rest with John (John 3.30), so it does not with the evangelist or teacher who is greatly used today.

The parable of the tenants (33–41) was addressed to the religious leaders of Israel, not to the people as a whole, who are represented by the vineyard (Isa. 5.1–7). Hence v. 43 is no statement about the Jewish people as such; it is, in fact, applicable to spiritual leaders in the Christian realm who imagine that they have achieved a certain autonomy by virtue of their position, which enables them to judge what is best for the Church, whatever the Scriptures may say. God is sovereign, and those who believe they can exercise sovereignty on His behalf often end up by rejecting Him and so are rejected. There is no adequate reason for omitting v. 44, cf. margin and Luke 20.18.

77 : The First Light of a New Day

John 12.20–50

The Greeks who wanted to see Jesus were Greek-speaking Gentiles of the type described in Acts as devout (10.2), worshippers of God (16.14), those that fear God (13.16); they attended the synagogue and kept the Noachic commandments (cf. Gen. 9.1–7), i.e. they avoided practices that made social contacts with Jews impossible, but they had not become proselytes, i.e. full Jews. Their approach to Philip of Bethsaida (21) suggests they were from the Decapolis. Their coming to Jerusalem for the Passover showed real devoutness, for they were not allowed further than the Court of the Gentiles—had they been attracted by Jesus' clearing out of the market?—and they were not allowed to share in the Passover meal (Exod. 12.48). A high proportion of the first Gentile Christians came from such circles.

John does not tell us the outcome of the request, though it is hard to believe it was refused; he is concerned that for Jesus it was the first ray of light at the end of the long 'valley of the shadow of death' He was entering. He had to die, but by death far more life could come—Paul uses the picture of the corn of wheat in a slightly different way (1 Cor. 15.36–38, 42–44). The way that Jesus went His disciples must follow (26).

The translation 'now is my soul troubled' (27) is somewhat misleading. In Hebraic thinking the soul is the whole man. With vs. 27 f. cf. the treatment of Matt. 26.36–56 (Study No. 81). It is often suggested that Jesus shrank from death, partly because of the shame of the cross, partly from what was involved in His becoming sin (or a sin offering, cf. 2 Cor. 5.21). Heb. 5.7 suggests that it was death itself that was the main load. To us who have 'to suffer the slings and arrows of outrageous fortune', who experience the decay of our bodies, who know that we *must* die, especially if we know we go to be with Christ, it is impossible to grasp what death meant to one who did not have to die. The lifting up (32, 34) was both crucifixion and exaltation.

In vs. 36b–41 we are introduced to a mystery of Divine activity, which receives fuller treatment in Rom. 9–11. Though the New Testament never plays down the guilt of the Jewish authorities, and to a lesser extent of the Jewish people, here above all it is made clear they were co-operating in a purpose they did not know; they could not believe (39). We cannot acquit them for their rejection and we should not dare to judge them. The repeated and strange blindness shown by the Church is probably only another example of the same thing.

78 : Jesus Faces His Enemies

Luke 20.19–21.4; Mark 12.28–34 (Matt. 22.15–23.36)

All three questions put to Jesus (Luke 20.21, 28; Mark 12.28) were intended to drive a wedge between Him and sections of the people. That they might have further results was secondary.

(a) The question about tribute money was intended to alienate His Zealot supporters, who (if our interpretation in Study No. 74 has been correct) had been mainly responsible for the Triumphal Entry. One of their principles was that loyalty to God made it impossible to recognize any other power. A 'No' would have made Him a revolutionary in the eyes of the Romans.

(b) The concept of resurrection had become part of the faith of the common people (John 11.24) largely because their conditions of life were so difficult. For Jesus to have been unable to defend it in the face of an obvious problem—the exaggerated question underlines the problem but does not create it—would have seriously discredited Him as a teacher. The question served as a swipe at the Pharisees as well.

(c) The scribe's question (Mark **12**.28) was more seriously meant, but he hoped to show that the establishment still stood above Jesus. In each case Jesus avoided the apparent dilemma by putting it in a different light or context. Whenever we face such dilemmas we can be sure they exist only because we see them out of focus.

Jesus riposted immediately by showing that His opponents had become so immersed in matters of secondary importance, points of law and theology, that they were unable to answer vital questions (Luke **20**.41–44). In spite of the varieties of Messianic expression, each group expected Him to conform to their concepts instead of realizing that He was coming as Lord. Then Jesus told the people to have a second look at the establishment (45–47, the full attack is in Matt. **23**.1–36). An establishment, religious and civil alike, becomes inflated by its position. It is very rare for the best man to reach the top, specially if Mark **10**.43 is his ideal. So we must constantly turn from the position to the man and his behaviour. It was not so much that they were bad—the devouring of widows' houses may have been the result of perfectly legal claims secured by due process of law (47)—but they were acting a part, which did not express their inner nature—the meaning of hypocrite in the New Testament.

The story of the widow's mite (**21**.1–4) owes its position not merely to chronological order but because it stands in such contrast to the members of the establishment just mentioned. What little work she did we are not told, but she earned less than a fiftieth of the standard day's wage, and she gave the whole of it.

79 : The Last Supper

Matthew 26.20–35 (Mark **14**.17–31; Luke **22**.14–38; 1 Cor. **11**.23–26)

The Passover lamb was sacrificed on Nisan 14 and eaten on Nisan 15, which began at sunset. Since no leaven was left after midday on Nisan 14, the Gospels call it 'the first day of Unleavened Bread' (Mark **14**.12; Matt. **26**.17). Owing to the continual use of the words of institution, in later manuscripts the various accounts have influenced one another. The cup of Luke **22**.17 is the first cup of the Passover meal. There can be little doubt that the announcement of the betrayal (21–25) took place during the meal itself and that Judas left when it was finished—he could not have left before. To this day the meal is followed by an epilogue, begun by a distribution of unleavened bread. It was then that Jesus said, 'This is my body, which is for you' (1 Cor. **11**.24—'given' or 'broken' is not found in the earliest manuscripts). To end this section of the epilogue the Cup of Blessing (1 Cor. **10**.16) is drunk. Jesus gave it with the words, 'This is the blood of the covenant which is poured out for many.' The next section of the epilogue ends with the singing of Pss. **115–118** (30). After this the fourth cup should have been drunk; it was omitted, because, unlike the Passover, which looks back, the Lord's Supper looks forward to the Lord's Coming (Luke **22**.18; 1 Cor. **11**.26).

Looking at the earliest form of the words of institution, it appears as if the bread points to the Bread of Life and Jesus' perfect life rather than to His death, just as the unleavened bread looked forward to new life rather than the delivering sacrifice, pictured by the wine. Had theologians considered that near the beginning of the Passover ceremony the celebrant displays the unleavened bread saying, 'This is the bread of affliction that our fathers ate in the land of Egypt', many would have hesitated to read a mystic meaning into our Lord's words. 'For many' (28) links with Mark **10**.45, and this in turn with Isa. **53**.12, where 'many' is a Hebrew way of saying 'all, and they are many', cf. Rom. **5**.18 f. Jesus' linking of His death with the Passover celebration is the clearest evidence of the sacrificial nature of His death.

Just as Judas could allow Satan to enter him when he ignored Jesus' love (John **13**.27), so Paul warns those who participate in the Lord's Supper without due regard for that love (1 Cor. **11**.27–30). Equally, Peter's denial, in spite of Jesus' warning, shows that the Supper should speak to us of our weakness and need.

80 : Love and Betrayal

John 13

John depicts Jesus as the Passover lamb, dying on the cross at the time the lambs were being sacrificed (**19**.14–16). Therefore he does not present the Last Supper as a Passover meal (1). The explanation of the apparent contradiction must be that in that year for some reason the Passover was celebrated on two days. The Synoptics agree with the popular majority, John with that of the Sadducean establishment, but the ritual of the Passover shines through his narrative.

We are not told whether the disciples had washed their feet when they entered the Upper Room. Between the ceremonial tasting of the Passover symbols and the main meal there is a purely ritual hand-washing, cf. Mark **7**.1–8. Instead of a meaningless act, Jesus, taking the part of a slave, washed His disciples' feet, a task considered so menial as to be forbidden by the rabbis to a Jewish slave. His explanation was that, at such a feast, it could be presumed that all had bathed, but their feet would be bound to be dusty from the road (10), the application of which is found in 1 John **1**.6 f. It formed, too, a lesson in humble service. The literal interpretation of v. 14 found in some Christian circles would be rejected by Jesus as being as meaningless today as the ritual hand-washing He had ignored. We fulfil it by obeying the new commandment (34). It was the old one (1 John **2**.7–9; Lev. **19**.18), given an entirely new content by Jesus' example.

Many are puzzled by the disciples' inability to grasp Jesus' plain words to and about Judas (26–29, cf. Matt. **26**.25). There are acts of such evil malignity, committed even by Christians, that we do not want to believe them possible. The other disciples could conceive the possibility of betrayal in the abstract (Matt. **26**.22), but the reality stunned them. That Judas was satisfied with thirty pieces of silver shows that gain was not his main purpose. Was it that he had trusted completely that Jesus would fulfil his deepest longings for Israel, and that when he saw that he would be disappointed, his love turned to hatred? At any rate he became the dwelling place of Satan (27). The man who cannot face the reality of sin denies both the existence of Satan and that Judas became completely evil (Matt. **26**.24).

The religious Jew prolongs the Passover feast deep into

the night, so there is no difficulty in fitting John **13–17** into the Synoptic story.

81 : Gethsemane

Matthew 26.36–56 (Mark **14**.32–50; Luke **22**.39–53; John **18**.1–12)

Jesus made careful preparations that He should not be disturbed during the Last Supper by ensuring that Judas did not know where it would be held (Mark **14**.12–16). After the meal, however, He went and waited for the betrayal in Gethsemane, which Judas knew well (Luke **22**.39; John **18**.2). The traditional translation of Jesus' feelings is too tame. Much better is the NEB 'horror and dismay came over Him' (Mark **14**.33; Phillips, 'horror-stricken and desperately distressed'), 'My heart is ready to break with grief' (38, NEB). Even for Jesus the future did not become completely real until it was the present. Not until the load of human sin with which He was identifying Himself, was settling on Him, could the sinless One fully grasp its terrible nature. For a moment He felt lost, for the sinner is lost.

An adequate answer to the charge that Christianity involves determinism is given by Jesus' prayer (Mark **14**.36). There has to be man's willingness to accept. Phillips and the TEV get the sense better with, 'not what I want, but what You want'. Jesus does not say '*your* flesh' but 'the flesh' (41). Not the shrinking but the unwillingness to accept God's will is sin.

It may seem strange that Judas allowed so much time to elapse, for we must allow ample time for John **14–17**, the walk to Gethsemane and the period of prayer. The authorities had decided to postpone the arrest until after the feast (**26**.5); it was only Judas' news that Jesus knew He was to be betrayed and was apparently awaiting arrest that stirred them to action. All this meant delay. In addition Judas may have gone to the Upper Room first—the lanterns and torches (John **18**.3) would not have been necessary in Gethsemane under the full moon. The degree of malignity in Judas' betrayal is seen in his greeting, 'Hail, Rabbi', and the kiss (49). It was held that the pupil owed special loyalty to his teacher. There are varying renderings of v. 50. The NEB follows the

RSV mg., which the TEV expresses excellently, 'Be quick about it, friend!' Judas was accomplishing God's purpose for Him, so Jesus had no hard words for him. Note that non-resistance does not exclude protest against wrong (55 f.).

Those who today justify violence in a 'just cause' should never forget v. 52; it remains true.

82 : Jesus before Caiaphas

Matthew 26.57–75 (Mark 14.53–72; Luke 22.54–71; John 18.13–27)

Today the view is often met that the trial story cannot be true because the behaviour of the Jewish court runs counter to the rules of procedure preserved in the Talmud. These are Pharisaic rules, demonstrably drawn up at a later date; at the time of Jesus justice was in Sadducean hands, and since the Pharisees considered them far too harsh, we need not doubt the truth of the judicial process described. The questioning before Annas (John 18.13, 19–24) was informal; Caiaphas was not yet available, for he was probably arranging next morning's trial with Pilate.

The witnesses were false (59) in the sense that they tried to present Jesus' words and acts in a false light; liars would have agreed. The one serious accusation was a twisted form of what Jesus had really said (61, John 2.19) but it was insufficient to justify a death sentence. Caiaphas' adjuration, 'In the name of the living God, I now put you on oath: tell us if you are the Messiah, the Son of God' (63, TEV), was contrary to every form of natural justice. In His answer (64) Jesus identified Himself with the Son of Man of Dan. 7.13, the coming ruler of the world, not only at the end of time but 'from now on' (NEB, Jer.B., TEV). Since Caiaphas could hardly have understood 'Son of God' in the Christian sense, the blasphemy was presumably the claim to be the Messiah before having demonstrated by actions His right to the title.

The Sanhedrin being far from complete at its night meeting, owing to its having been so hurriedly convened, its decision was confirmed at a fuller meeting at dawn (Luke 22.66–71).

It is usually assumed that John was the disciple who

enabled Peter to enter Caiaphas' palace (John **18**.15 f.). Probably the maid at the door had no malice behind her statement (69), but it made Peter feel suddenly that he had entered the lion's den. Once having denied it was hard to confess. The translations of v. 74 and Mark **14**.71 may well be too charitable to Peter; it was probably on Jesus that Peter was calling down the curses as proof positive. The mention of the double cock-crow in Mark **14**.30, 72, as against the single one in the other Gospels, goes back to Peter himself.

83 : The Crucifixion

John 19.1–37 (Matt. **27**.24–50; Mark **15**.15–37; Luke **23**.24–46)

Pilate's position, in one way, was like Peter's. He was not obliged to try Jesus; once he decided to he had sufficient secret service information to discharge Him at once, but once he hesitated he was lost. In vs. 1–16 we have his last despairing, unavailing attempts to extricate himself. The Jewish authorities too were carried away by the tide; they had never expected to acknowledge Caesar as king (15). 'The Jews', as so often in John, are the religious leaders. The only role the people played centred in Barabbas (Mark **15**.6–15). The fiery nationalists felt that Jesus had let them down; if they had to choose between Him and Barabbas, they considered the latter had more to offer them. The contrast often drawn between the Triumphal Entry and 'Crucify!' is often ill-conceived. They had hailed Him then not for what He was but for what they thought Him to be.

John, writing after the Synoptics, and so leaving other details to them, confines himself to a picture of the King, all hesitation past, going serenely to His throne on the cross. Three times we find Scripture mentioned as being fulfilled. The soldiers blindly carried out Psa. **22**.18 (24). Note that though the Synoptics mention the division, they do not link it with the psalm. It was not invented, as the sceptic maintains, to provide a fulfilment. Then Jesus deliberately provided a fulfilment of Scripture in quoting Psa. **69**.21, thereby linking Himself with all who suffer for righteousness' sake. Finally, God overruled the disposal of His body, that He might be seen to be the true Passover lamb (36). This looks forward to the fulfilment of Zech. **12**.10, cf. Rev. **1**.7.

John stresses that out of Jesus' spear-pierced side came blood and water, cf. 1 John **5**.6. Medically, the meaning is disputed. Spiritually, we can be certain that John was meeting the view of many contemporaries that Jesus did not really die and was not fully man. Then, too, though 'the blood of Jesus Christ' means His death, John saw His blood poured out like that of the sacrificial animals. The water speaks of His purifying power. As Toplady wrote:

> Let the water and the blood,
> From Thy riven side which flowed,
> Be of sin the double cure—
> Cleanse me from its guilt and pow'r.

Questions and themes for study and discussion on Studies 74-83

1. From the time of Peter's confession at Caesarea Philippi Jesus sought to show His disciples what *kind* of Messiah He had come to be. How would the events of Palm Sunday help this educative process?

2. The Temple was twice cleansed, but why has God given us a record of both occasions?

3. Can we tell whether a miracle is from God or Satan?

4. What anticipations of the extension of the gospel to the Gentiles do we find in the ministry of Jesus?

5. Study the wisdom of Jesus on the Day of Questions.

6. Why do you think Jesus instituted the Lord's Supper?

7. What place is there for symbolic acts in the life of the Christian?

8. Was the experience in Gethsemane necessary? Does it make His sacrifice at Calvary even more meaningful?

9. How could a religious leader employ liars and reject the very Son of God?

10. Why is John especially emphatic about the water and the blood?

CHARACTER STUDIES

84 : Valiant Youth

Daniel 1; 1 Corinthians 10.23–33

It was a traumatic experience to be dragged into captivity at the beginning of manhood, and it must have seemed to them unbelievable good fortune when some of the young men were set aside to be used as leaders in the cosmopolitan empire which the king was seeking to build. The shrewd Nebuchadnezzar was looking for able civil servants, and the pressure on those chosen for such training to conform to the pagan world into which they were introduced must have been overwhelming.

The names of the boys all contained the name of their God, 'iah' and 'el'. 'Daniel' means 'God is my judge'; Hananiah means 'God is gracious'; Mishael means 'Who is as God'; Azariah means 'God has helped'. The meaning of Belteshazzar is doubtful, but it probably means 'Protect his life'. According to the lexicon Shadrach is also of doubtful meaning, while Meshach may simply mean 'Who is this?' and Abednego may mean 'Servant of Nabu' with the 'b' changed to 'g' to slur the offensive name of the pagan deity.

Thus it often goes with the world. Pagan society is content, as a preliminary step, if it can get the divine syllable out of the Christian's 'name'. It does not at first concentrate on substituting the gods of heathendom. Daniel, in his strong maturity, was aware of this. What others called him did not matter. What he did in person to aid the process of absorption was what concerned him. There he could stand firm.

The law had said much of food. It was a symbol in the Hebrew code, and Daniel saw the food of Babylon as a sign of pagan living, and its acceptance an act of surrender. In the practice of contemporary society there are features which, perhaps harmless in themselves, have assumed the nature of a test, like the 'meat sacrificed to idols' in Corinth. To participate, accept, or to partake becomes, for the Christian, an act of compromise, and a demonstration of conformity.

Daniel and his friends decided to be separate, an act of

114

valour under the circumstances. They no doubt received much contrary advice, much warning of perilous imprudence, much angry protest among those afraid to be involved in the minority's intransigence. They stood firm, left career and safety in God's hands, refused to accept the symbols of paganism, and were richly vindicated.

85 : Nebuchadnezzar

Daniel 2

The king of Babylon has haunted the background of many of our studies, a peril from the north, a sinister visitant, a harbinger of death. Now we meet him in person, a cruel, unreasonable, capricious tyrant. 'Uneasy lies the head that wears a crown,' said Shakespeare, and how truly! Nebuchadnezzar was drunk with power. Such minds are not at ease. Fear of assassination haunts them, and their suppressed suspicions and hatreds, rampant during day, emerge at night to murder sleep.

Savagely the king commanded his soothsayers to recall the dream, which had left only a dark dread behind, and to tell the meaning. None of them dared say that the problem which he sought to solve was the evil in his own heart. Fierce punishment, extravagant reward, injustice, caprice are the manifestations of tyranny. Observe now the quiet, brave manhood which was to confront the raving tyrant. Daniel's youthful self-discipline made the courageous man.

He sought the wisdom of God, and was granted his prayer. In two ways he showed himself worthy of such grace. He must have despised the wizardry and fortune-telling of the 'wise men' of Babylon, but he sought, in humanity, to save them from the punishment of the king. His first reaction to answered prayer was gratitude, and a beautiful prayer of worship followed (20–23). Too often we are ready enough with our prayers of petition, but slow to utter the prayer of gratitude and praise. In the presence of the king, Daniel claimed no special wisdom. He gave God all the glory, and sought occasion, in the service he rendered, to commend the God he worshipped. The portraiture of Daniel never varies, for there was no variety in the front he presented to the world. Two great qualities stand out: his deep reverence for God, and his fearless demeanour before men. Before God he bowed the knee; before men he stood erect and unafraid. And in his eyes Nebuchadnezzar was no more than man, to be treated with the respect his rank demanded, but with no trace of servility or flattery.

The imagery of the king's dream was probably allowed to arise from his own fears, apprehensions, and experience. Such great statues, wrought in all manner of material, stood in his courts. It was easy for him to imagine himself the exalted head, priceless and uplifted. And such was the meaning borne by the head of gold. The vast and ill-knit empire provided the rest of his dream material. It sprawled across the Middle East, its many parts cast together by conquest and with small coherence. To fit the subsequent details to any known patterns of history is a precarious process and need not detain us. It is the insight into the royal mind which makes the interest of the dream—this self-image of a colossus, most precariously standing.

86 : Royal Rage

Daniel 3

'You will be like God' was part of the first temptation, and it has always been the last folly and corruption of man to set himself in the place of God. The Pharaohs of Egypt and the Emperors of Rome indulged this blasphemy, either in the arrogance of self-delusion or in the harshness of tyranny and its cynical statecraft. The virus of such absurd but perilous evil has not been purged from the spirit of man, as the exaltation of political leaders in our own age has grimly demonstrated. Pride is a basic ingredient in all sin, and Nebuchadnezzar in this story shows sinful pride in its ultimate folly.

There are few spurs to anger sharper than wounded pride. In perpetual fear of all independence, and more and more in need of proof of men's servility and obedience, the king was wild with rage at the report of the Jews' refusal to worship. The sight was absurd, but fraught with danger. Human life meant nothing to the tyrant of Babylon. Perhaps hostile elements in Babylon saw with jealousy the rise to influence, and perhaps affluence of groups of intelligent Jews, and sought to stir the royal wrath against them. This was to happen in Esther's day. It happened in Rome in A.D. 64 when Nero rose to kill the Christians.

That violence and ungovernable excess which were the mark of the king's corrupted character are evident in this story. His very face was ravaged and distorted by rage as he cast his former favourites down and condemned them to a horrible death. God intervened and they were preserved. On many other occasions He has not intervened and evil has had its way. There is inexplicable sovereignty in such intervention.

Observe now the wild excesses to which the proud arrogance of the man was prone. He decreed horrible punishment for all who should refuse worship to the God of Daniel. God requires no such worship, nor seeks such champions as the passionate king. Those who bring others to His feet must do so with persuasion of word and deed. Those who come must come with understanding, with willingness, with humility and surrender. Man's patronage of God must be ultimate irony.

87 : Messenger of Truth

Daniel 4.1–27; Ezekiel 2.3–10

The dream again reveals the man, and shows the unseen stresses and strains which led to his mental catastrophe. The king of Babylon was haunted by many fears. His will was supreme, but he lived in daily apprehension of a challenge to it. Hence his wild wrath when any man thwarted him. Hence, too, his need to reassure himself by the visible worship of the multitudes. No man violates divine law without producing tension in the mind, and it is not the will of God that one man should hold millions in his power, and deal out capriciously life and death, reward and disaster. Such might usurps the power of God, feeds ruinous pride, and perverts the personality. The king, too, was not without some knowledge of God. His accession prayer is extant. It shows understanding of spiritual things. Hence the tangle in his soul, and the deep, hidden layer of self-distrust in his mind, a fear of a fall which he strove desperately to hide. It was of such concealed terrors that his dream was made. It was built out of the stuff of life. Nor is this to say that it was not implanted of God. God was to send judgement on the despot, but chose to warn him, for it was not His purpose at this time to destroy the kingdom.

Daniel was aghast at what he saw to be the meaning of the king's dream. He knew the wild passions of the man with whom he had to deal, and might very naturally have felt daunted at the duty of speaking the truth which he saw before him. And yet he also saw reason in the warning. All power was to pass from the king for full seven years, long enough to bring ruin on Babylon, and on the people of Daniel, who lay under the shadow of 'the great tree'. Giving warning, it might be possible so to dispose of the essentials of power and government that order might survive the loss of the absolute authority which ruled the land. Daniel therefore spoke up, and spoke the truth. It was said of Samuel that he delivered faithfully the message of God. Whatever the consequences, however sinister the peril, the man who is entrusted with the truth of God dare do no less than boldly proclaim it. Only thus, as was said to Ezekiel, is the truth faithfully proclaimed and the herald vindicated.

88 : Mad King

Daniel 4.28–37

Few men have held wider power than Nebuchadnezzar of Babylon. It was no idle boast he made one evening on his palace roof when he looked across the greatest city of the ancient world and cried: 'Is not this great Babylon, which I have built by my mighty power . . . ?' It is a fact that half the bricks in the mighty ruins by the Euphrates are stamped with his name. He had the building mania of all such despotic characters. And from the summit of his pride and self-exaltation he tumbled and touched the very bedrock of despair. He rushed to the palace lawns and tore grass with his teeth, imagining himself to be an ox.

This great conqueror and megalomaniac, demanding divine honours, was also a man prone to piety. It is, psychologically, a very likely personality which we thus can see. Further, such types are subject to the mental malady of melancholia. The

118

sufferers plunge from self-exaltation to despair, are vague about their identity, humiliate and torture themselves, and often, strangel: enough, recover suddenly with complete memory of their mental sufferings. It is a disease of high places. Richelieu, mighty minister of Louis XIII of France, imagined on occasion that he was a horse. It is also a disease of the basically pious. Richelieu, for all the corruption of his religion, was a cardinal of the Church. Nebuchadnezzar set high store by divine things. Often, too, religion clears such clouded minds. It saved the king of Babylon.

Authorities on mental disorder say that this is a commonly observed phenomenon. One says: 'The king's remembrance of the circumstances of his degradation is not remarkable. Patients are often able to tell what was their mental state prior to their madness and some are able to describe the whole course of their delusions.' Nebuchadnezzar knew that wild self-exaltation had dethroned his reason and thereafter was a better man. His madness had been purgatorial. Again, madness was looked upon as a visitation from God. The throne would be waiting for the restored king, protected during his lunacy by the awe which in those times always attached itself to the mentally deranged. The exact picture impresses with a sense of its historical reality.

89 : Belshazzar

Daniel 5

This superbly written chapter tells the tale of a dissolute royal feast and a scene of uncanny judgement. It was October, 539 B.C. Whose fingers did they see writing on the plaster of the wall those cryptic words which Daniel interpreted? Did each carnal banqueter see his own hand-writing, that characteristic crook of thumb and forefinger, that intimate trick of the stilus which each man and woman knew? Men do write their own doom, and Babylon was dying of no obscure disease that night. It was passing because the sin of men, as the Hebrew prophets saw, had sapped its life. It was passing with the evil of its king. Belshazzar had seen Nebuchadnezzar judged for his mad pride and had seen insanity fall upon him. He had seen the wisdom of Daniel applied in the councils of state, but now Daniel was forgotten, and blasphemy reigned in the palace halls. He was beyond excuse . . .

'To the vast mound of Babylon,' wrote Layard, one of the first modern travellers to visit the site, 'succeed long undulating heaps of bricks and pottery. Other shapeless heaps of rubbish cover for many an acre the face of the land. On all sides fragments of glass, marble and inscribed brick are mingled with that peculiar nitrous and blanched soil, which, bred from the remains of ancient habitations, destroys vegetation and renders the site of Babylon a naked and hideous waste. Owls start from the scanty thickets, and the foul jackal skulks through the furrows.'

'And Babylon,' wrote Isaiah, almost two centuries earlier, 'the glory of kingdoms, the splendour and pride of the Chaldeans, will be like Sodom and Gomorrah when God overthrew them. It will never be inhabited, or dwelt in for all generations; no Arab will pitch his tent there . . . But wild beasts will lie down there, and its houses will be full of howling creatures . . . hyenas will cry in its towers, and jackals in the pleasant palaces . . .' (Isa. **13**.19–22). How aptly the descriptions tally!

Daniel, the magnificent figure of that night of doom, survived. As his nation, set amid the clashing empires, survived them all, so the Hebrew prisoner of Babylon bridged the eras of Babylon. No compromise preserved his life. There were lesser Jews, like Esther and Mordecai of a later year, who came to terms with the pagan environment, and bought life at too dear a cost. Daniel was of the ancestry of Nehemiah and Ezra, in whose hands the future of all history lay. The future lay not even with the Medes and Persians, who at that moment were turning aside the river, and making a road through the walls of Babylon.

90 : Man of God

Daniel 6

Verse 5 is the most magnificent tribute a man can win. If a hostile, jealous, watching world can discover nothing against a man save his devotion to his God, that man is truly Christlike. The Lord Himself, alone of men, could look with steady eyes at His foes and ask. 'Which of you convicts me of sin?' No mortal being can put such a challenge into words; but if life can be so nobly lived that the world has to admit that it cannot point its scornful finger at conduct and character, then something of Christ's glory has found reflection in the testimony. Every sphere of life—business, sport, social intercourse, political activity—is related to our witness for the Lord. In all these places the Christian is watched critically and appraisingly, his deeds measured against his profession, his words weighed. To pass a scrutiny so searching, sometimes so unjust, often malign, is a task for care, diligence, forbearance, patience, self-control, complete humility, and, above all, 'watching unto prayer' . . .

No nation, no man, has a monopoly of folly. The human race is one in its acquaintance with sin. In the experience of all centuries and all nations, we are brothers under the skin. We have seen the megalomania and the insane pride of Nebuchadnezzar. We shall meet the vicious Ahasuerus. Darius was the victim of the same corruption. 'Power corrupts,' in Lord Acton's well-known saying, 'and absolute power corrupts absolutely.' We have had illustrations enough in this century. As we read this story we are made aware of two miracles. Daniel survived his awful ordeal by the mercy of One who 'stopped the mouths of lions,' as another Jew of the Dispersion wrote six centuries later (Heb. 11.33). But the favour and standing he held in the eyes of the capricious, cruel monarch was a miracle as great. God sometimes provides His children with such aid, and causes the pagan world to serve Him. There is no pattern by which such mercy may be measured. Too often hatred and the lions have had their way, and death has been permitted by One who must view death with other eyes than ours. At other times His hand thrusts evil back, and that may most justly be our prayer.

91 : Daniel the Prophet

Daniel 9.1–19; 10.1–14

There is nothing more natural than that the fall of the Babylonian Empire should turn Daniel to the searching of the Scriptures for the significance of historical events. The Book of the Revelation has come into its own again in many lands in these apocalyptic days. And note that the study of Scripture inevitably turns the devout mind to prayer. Daniel's prayer holds a solemn place in the collection of the great prayers of the Bible. It is alive and aglow with the fire of genuine repentance, assured faith, and intense petition. Like Jeremiah, Daniel, as we have seen, reveals Christlike features. He was not blameworthy in the backslidings of Israel. He had kept the faith in all perils, and at all costs. And yet, vicariously, he took the sins of his people upon himself, and suffered for them. The prayer is full of Scripture, as are always the prayers of those who have lived much with the Word of God. To pray in the words of God is to move close to prevailing prayer. It should be compared, as a devotional exercise, with the prayers of Ezra and Nehemiah. Ezra confesses the sins of his people without asking for forgiveness (Ezra 9.6–15). Nehemiah praises God, but does not cry for pardon (Neh. 1.4–11). Daniel stresses the petition which both of the others omit.

Since it was the third year of Cyrus (10.1) when Daniel had his mystic experience, it is clear that he did not return to Jerusalem with Zerubbabel. There was a ministry to be exercised among the less valiant Jews who had elected to stay in foreign parts. It is well for most people that God does not abandon those of His children who fail to follow as closely as they should. Were there such limits on His care—'how helpless and hopeless we sinners had been!'' Perhaps the theme of Daniel's deep exercise of soul was this very problem. Should he remain in Babylon, doubtless to be misunderstood and criticized by the more zealous? Or should he go, as his heart probably dictated, to aid in the rebuilding of the land and witness? He had remained for a period at his post but, perhaps, as the third year opened a crisis of doubt came to him and, as a devout soul does at such a time, he sought God's will. For three weeks he found no clarity or peace. And then God revealed Himself. Like Moses, Job, Isaiah, and Peter, Daniel's first reaction was to confess to his own unworthiness.

Questions and themes for study and discussion on Studies 84-91

1. Arrogance, pride and mental stability.
2. Christians and high office. Is it to be sought?

3. Faith and healing of the mind.
4. With whom does the future of history lie today?
5. Is there any 'writing on the wall' today?
6. 'Dare to be a Daniel.'
7. How are we 'weighed in the balances'? Against what?
8. How does the world try to change our names?
9. What basic elements of prayer can you distinguish in Daniel's prayer?

THE LIFE OF CHRIST

The Resurrection and Ascension

92 : The First at the Tomb

John 20.1–23 (Matt. **28**.1–10; Mark **16**.1–8; Luke **24**.1–12)

It is comparatively easy to weave the four narratives of Jesus' trial and death into one, but this is really impossible with the resurrection story. It is as though the apostles took great care that the narrative of their Lord's death should raise no questions by seeming contradictions. With the resurrection, however, the shout is, 'We have seen Him; He is alive for evermore!', and so the individuality of personal experience receives its full expression.

The use of 'we' (2) shows that there is no conflict with Matt. **28**.1; Mark **16**.1. In all versions of the story great stress is laid on the stone. This is usually pictured as one in the shape of a wheel, moving in a groove. The use of such stones was rarer than generally assumed, and the language fits a boulder moved into position at least as well, cf. Matt. **28**.2; with such a stone the anxiety of the women is easy to understand. What Peter and John saw was the grave-cloths, long linen strips, still maintaining, thanks to the spices, the shape of the body, and the cloth that had been around His head, where it had rested. The resurrection body of Jesus had passed out of the burial cloths and tomb. The stone had been rolled away that men might see the tomb was empty; the cloths had been guarded by the angel (Matt. **28**.5) that the two disciples might see them untouched and so believe (8). The comment in v. 9 means that they should have believed, but did not, on the basis of the Old Testament alone.

To each according to his need: for John the grave-cloths sufficed, for heart-broken Mary the personal revelation, for Peter a meeting so intimate that no more than its fact is told (1 Cor. **15**.5; Luke **24**.34). Let us never try to force our relationship with the living Lord into a fixed pattern. Jesus would never have denied Mary (17) what He offered Thomas (27), so the AV is badly at fault; the RSV 'hold' is adequate, but the best is 'Do not cling to me' (NEB, Jer. B.).

Jesus prepared the ones He loved most carefully (by His earlier appearances) for His first group appearance. There were more than the Eleven present (Luke 24.33, 36), a fact of importance for our understanding of vs. 22 f. If Jesus' eating (Luke 24.41 f.) was a mark of loving condescension, it is reasonable to think that the marks of the nails and spear were equally so, the more so as the other marks of the passion are not mentioned. Doubtless those who would feel that something were missing in heaven without them will see them there also.

93 : The Road to Emmaus

Luke 24.13–43

Though the story of Jesus' joining a pair of dispirited disciples on their way home to Emmaus is a favourite one, we seldom ask ourselves why this otherwise unknown pair—was the unnamed one Cleopas' wife?—was granted a privilege apparently given to no others. If, as seems probable, they lived in Emmaus, they belonged to the relatively small number of Judeans who had put their trust in Jesus. They had not been able to hear His Galilean teaching, and though they lived only seven miles from Jerusalem, they could easily miss much that was happening there. As said before, 'To each according to his need'.

There is here an interesting repetition. Not merely to the two on the road (27) but also to the larger company in the upper room (44–47) Jesus went through the Old Testament, explaining the prophetic statements about Himself. This is recorded by Luke as a claim that the Christian treatment of the Old Testament, often strange to the Jew and foolish to the modern expositor, was in fact derived from Jesus Himself. To say this is not to justify the forcing of Old Testament texts to bear an impossible Messianic meaning, which is still often met. If we look at the New Testament evidence more closely, we shall see that its writers are normally more concerned with Old Testament *passages* than individual texts; when these are quoted they often point to their context as a whole.

We are assured here that Jesus' resurrection body was a real one (39). It is highly improbable that the non-mention of blood is significant. At the same time the body was under the influence of spirit in a way we can only dimly understand. The concept of 'psychosomatic' has become a commonplace in modern medicine, both for sickness and health, but those using it do not know how it works. We are not granted the powers of physical transformation possessed by our Lord, but we do have the spirit transforming us from glory to glory (2 Cor. **3**.17 f.). This does not mean that we should be free from illness and physical weakness, as some maintain, but that, when they come, they can be welcomed as God's will.

'While they still disbelieved for joy' (41); this is an element for which we do not always allow. The gospel is so wonderful, that some on hearing it genuinely fear disappointment, especially when they see Christian lives falling short of it.

94 : My Lord and my God

John 20.24–31

Thomas was one of those who disbelieved for joy. A natural pessimist, he was absolutely devoted to Jesus (**11**.16). It may well have been the depth of his sorrow that kept him from the fellowship of his companions (24). The very vehemence of his words—'I refuse to believe' (Jer. B.) gives the sense better—betrays his desire to be convinced. Once again we have an example of 'To each according to his need.' It is highly improbable that he availed himself of Jesus' invitation, but the graciousness and super-human knowledge displayed by Jesus swept him to his knees with the glad cry, 'My Lord and my God.'

Thomas was a devout Jew for whom the existence of only one God was axiomatic. Had he been challenged to justify his words intellectually, he could not have done so, but he would not have retracted them. The belief in the deity of Jesus Christ and the resultant doctrine of the Trinity are not the fruit of some theoretical theology, but the only possible expression of our experience of His saving and transforming power. This should always be remembered, when we speak to Jews, Muslims, some heretical sectarians and atheists. We preach a crucified and risen Christ. If they come to know Him, the rest will follow also.

It is not only in New Testament times that man has experienced 'To each according to his need'. Today also many are tempted to feel despondent, when they hear ecstatic testimonies to marvellous experiences of Divine grace, with whatever label they may be named. It is then that we should remember 'Blessed are those who have not seen and yet believe'. Very often those who receive such outstanding signs of Divine love are babes who cannot walk by faith but need sight. It is Divine love that enables many to walk without sight, and blessed are they.

Just as the evangelists left much unrecorded (30), so these comments have passed over much in silence, and for the same reason. Anything that does not create deeper faith that Jesus is the Messiah, God's King, and lead to discipleship has little value for the normal Christian, however true it may be, and however much it may be useful to the Christian apologist.

95 : The Ascension

Matthew 28.16–20; Luke 24.44–53

Ever since Jesus Christ ascended to heaven the Church has been demonstrating His power by its walk of faith. To a very few He has, for a brief moment, vouchsafed a fleeting vision of Himself, but for the rest the Christian walk has been by means of the unseen and often unfelt influence of the Holy Spirit making Him and His will real. Under the influence of the modern demythologizer the story of the Ascension is scorned, but so long as man remains within the space-time continuum, which conditions our experiences of nature, there was no other way in which it could be made clear to His disciples and to us, that Jesus Christ had passed with His perfect manhood and resurrection body to a mode of existence of which we know nothing, there to rule until every enemy is put under His feet.

The story in Matt. 28.16–20 is probably that referred to in 1 Cor. 15.6. The Eleven will not have been among the doubters, but only they are mentioned to make it clear that Jesus' command was one to the Church, which is built on their teaching (Eph. 2.20). There are rare cases where someone must go out completely alone, but normally there should be co-operation between church and individual, cf. Acts 13.1–3. We cannot claim the promise of Christ's presence (20) unless we are where He wants us to be.

We always long to make a completely new beginning, to cut off the disastrous past, but not so God. Jerusalem and its temple were already under the sentence of destruction (Luke 19.41–44), but it had to be from there that the gospel went out first. Today also, unless we are prepared to make the gospel credible where we are called (1 Cor. 7.24), we are not likely to make it so where we are unknown.

One feature of the Primitive Church is its apparent lack of urgency—urgency and intensity are different matters. The initial command to wait (Luke 24.49) was realized to be more than a mere waiting for the Holy Spirit. Acts is full of stories showing how God opened new doors when the time was ripe. Equally, the Son of God waited thirty years in Nazareth being prepared. When God has taught us the lessons we have to learn, He will move us without delay.

Questions and themes for study and discussion on Studies 92-95

1. The disciples saw the actual moment of the ascension. Does it matter that they did not see the actual moment of the resurrection?

2. What Old Testament passages do you think would have figured in that wonderful discourse on the road to Emmaus?

3. If we have not seen and yet believe, is our faith blind or does it have some basis of knowledge other than physical sight?

4. Does the Great Commission still apply?